In the Wreckage of ISIS

An Examination of Challenges Confronting Detained
and Displaced Populations in Northeastern Syria

KAREN M. SUDKAMP, NATHAN VEST, ERIK E. MUELLER,
TODD C. HELMUS

Prepared for the Office of the Secretary of Defense
Approved for public release; distribution unlimited

 NATIONAL DEFENSE RESEARCH INSTITUTE

For more information on this publication, visit **www.rand.org/t/RRA471-1**.

About RAND

The RAND Corporation is a research organization that develops solutions to public policy challenges to help make communities throughout the world safer and more secure, healthier and more prosperous. RAND is nonprofit, nonpartisan, and committed to the public interest. To learn more about RAND, visit www.rand.org.

Research Integrity

Our mission to help improve policy and decisionmaking through research and analysis is enabled through our core values of quality and objectivity and our unwavering commitment to the highest level of integrity and ethical behavior. To help ensure our research and analysis are rigorous, objective, and nonpartisan, we subject our research publications to a robust and exacting quality-assurance process; avoid both the appearance and reality of financial and other conflicts of interest through staff training, project screening, and a policy of mandatory disclosure; and pursue transparency in our research engagements through our commitment to the open publication of our research findings and recommendations, disclosure of the source of funding of published research, and policies to ensure intellectual independence. For more information, visit www.rand.org/about/research-integrity.

RAND's publications do not necessarily reflect the opinions of its research clients and sponsors.

About This Report

The territorial defeat of the Islamic State of Iraq and Syria (ISIS) left millions of Iraqi and Syrian civilians displaced, along with the families of Syrian, Iraqi, and foreign ISIS fighters. A significant share of the families of ISIS fighters resides in two camps located in Syria, al-Hol and Roj, intermingled with Syrian and Iraqi civilians. There are open questions about the futures of the residents of these camps and the implications of housing innocent, displaced residents alongside or adjacent to the families of ISIS fighters. One of the most-significant challenges of this arrangement is the need to limit the spread of extremist ideology and ISIS recruitment among the children of ISIS fighters' families and other civilians.

In this report, we examine the humanitarian and security conditions in these camps, address the potential impact on ISIS recruitment, and highlight critical challenges in the need to return these displaced residents to their home communities and countries. We also offer recommendations to improve living conditions in al-Hol and Roj, address the legal and judicial conundrums facing foreigners living in the camps, and mitigate the threat of radicalization from the residents within the camps. This report should be of interest to U.S. defense and diplomatic policymakers, their European counterparts, and partners in the United Nations and international nongovernmental organizations who are focused on providing support to refugees and internally displaced persons.

The research reported here was completed in September 2021 and underwent security review with the sponsor and the Defense Office of Prepublication and Security Review before public release.

Human Subject Protections (HSP) protocols were used in this study in accordance with the appropriate statutes and U.S. Department of Defense (DoD) regulations governing HSP. Additionally, the views of the sources rendered anonymous by HSP are solely their own and do not represent the official policy or position of DoD or the U.S. government.

RAND National Security Research Division

This research was conducted within the International Security and Defense Policy Program of the RAND National Security Research Division (NSRD), which operates the RAND National Defense Research Institute (NDRI), a federally funded research and development center (FFRDC) sponsored by the Office of the Secretary of Defense, the Joint Staff, the Unified Combatant Commands, the Navy, the Marine Corps, the defense agencies, and the defense intelligence enterprise. This research was made possible by NDRI exploratory research funding that was provided through the FFRDC contract and approved by NDRI's primary sponsor.

For more information on the RAND International Security and Defense Policy Program, see www.rand.org/nsrd/isdp or contact the director (contact information is provided on the webpage).

Acknowledgments

We are grateful to the leadership of RAND's National Security Research Division and the International Security and Defense Policy Program who helped make funding available for this research. We are also grateful to many experts who participated in interviews and whose observations and insights formed a basis for this research. We thank Shelly Culbertson of the RAND Corporation and Michael "Mick" Mulroy of the Lobo Institute for their helpful and careful reviews of this report. We also want to thank Doug Ligor for his insights into international migration law and recommendations on the language about the legal categorizations of camp inhabitants. Finally, we thank Lauren Skrabala and Katie Hynes for their assistance in preparing this report for publication.

Summary

Syria's decade-long civil war has caused a displacement crisis that affects every corner of the country, with Kurdish-controlled northeastern Syria grappling with a unique set of displacement challenges. Multiple waves of displacement have brought a variety of populations to the camps for internally displaced persons (IDPs) and refugees in northeastern Syria, including Syrians, Iraqis, and foreign nationals. Displaced Syrian civilians represent about a third of those residing in these camps, a consequence of both the Syrian Civil War and the campaign to territorially defeat the Islamic State of Iraq and Syria (ISIS). This group likely includes those with ISIS affiliations. More than half of camp residents in the region are Iraqi civilians—those persecuted by ISIS—and ISIS families. These displacements have overwhelmed IDP and refugee camps in the region, especially Ain Issa, al-Hol, and Roj. In the latter half of 2020 alone, an estimated 700,000 individuals remained displaced by the conflict across the Kurdish-controlled areas of Syria.[1]

In addition to the customary humanitarian and security responsibilities related to sheltering and protecting displaced populations, the northeastern Syrian camps face an additional challenge: More than 40,000 women and children with actual or perceived ties to ISIS fighters have arrived at the camps seeking shelter and now live alongside civilians who fled ISIS rule in Iraq and Syria. Both al-Hol and Roj host substantial foreign populations, including Westerners, and many of the camps' residents lived under ISIS control for years; some still promulgate the group's ideology. We undertook this research to assess the humanitarian and security situation in the camps—particularly al-Hol and Roj. In the process, we examine how continued displacement in a setting characterized by hardship and a mixing of civilians with ISIS followers and the families of ISIS fighters could affect the risk of radicalization among the camps' populations and the risk of an ISIS resurgence in northeastern Syria. Table S.1 shows the three primary categories of camp residents—IDPs (Syrians), refugees (Iraqis), and foreigners—

---

[1] United Nations Office for the Coordination of Humanitarian Affairs, "Syrian Arab Republic NES Displacement Returns 18 Dec 2019," December 29, 2019b; Médecins Sans Frontières, "'In Al-Hol Camp, Almost No Healthcare Is Available,'" August 27, 2020.

TABLE S.1

Categories of Residents in the Northeastern Syrian Camps and Key Issues

Country of Origin	Category and Key Issues	Estimated Presence

Syria	IDPs
	• have fled fighting from both the Syrian Civil War and the counter-ISIS campaign
	  – potentially unsafe for these populations to return home, where they could face persecution by the Syrian regime
	• almost certainly includes ISIS-affiliated individuals
	  – lack of justice processes to collect evidence and prosecute
		20,600[a]

Iraq	Refugees
	• predominately fled fighting the counter-ISIS campaign, including minorities persecuted by ISIS
	  – cannot be forced to return to Iraq
	  – broad assumption by Iraqi politicians and population that they are ISIS-affiliated
	• almost certainly includes ISIS-affiliated individuals
	  – lack of justice processes to collect evidence and prosecute
		30,800

Foreign countries[b]	Undetermined
	• assumed to be predominately ISIS-affiliated
	  – lack of justice processes to collect evidence and prosecute
	  – home countries lack the political will to repatriate, collect evidence to prosecute, or leverage broad legal authorities and resources to maintain oversight over this population
		11,200

[a] The estimated 26,300 Syrian IDPs include Syrians at al-Hol and Roj only.

[b] The contingent of foreign families in al-Hol represents more than 60 different countries; citizens of each country face a different repatriation process.

and associated policy barriers that have prevented them from being repatriated to their home countries or communities.[2]

---

[2] All data used for this report were current as of June 2021 and were not updated prior to the release of the report.

We examined relevant literature that included journal articles, government and think tank reports, and media articles to develop a picture of the humanitarian situation and the presence and reach of ISIS in the camps. We complemented this research with 14 not-for-attribution interviews with officials from the U.S. government, human rights and refugee support organizations, and Kurdish governmental organizations to receive the most-updated information about the situation in the camps and their understanding of the presence and activity of ISIS within the camps. We also reviewed literature on factors that influence radicalization more broadly and variables among refugee and displaced populations that might leave them vulnerable to militancy. Finally, we reviewed case studies of conflicts over the past 30 years that resulted in significant displacement of civilians.

Policy Implications and Recommendations

The al-Hol and Roj camps present both monumental humanitarian challenges and a significant security concern, given the camp residents' vulnerability to exploitation by armed groups. Indefinite policy inaction on al-Hol and Roj is not a durable solution to the crisis that is mounting in northeastern Syria and could lead to a resurgence of ISIS.

The recommendations that follow are intended to guide decisions by the United States, European countries, the United Nations, the Autonomous Administration of North and East Syria (AANES), and Syrian Democratic Forces (SDF), along with the nongovernmental organizations (NGOs) with which they partner. These recommendations include both potential avenues to improve humanitarian and security conditions at the camps and steps to support successful repatriation of displaced populations and long-term security in the region.

Allowing residents of refugee and IDP camps to remain in an indefinite holding pattern could increase their vulnerability to radicalization or enable an ISIS resurgence. The vast majority of residents at al-Hol, for example—possibly up to 94 percent—are women and children. Foreigners are housed in a separate annex, and their murky legal status has potential implications for their access to services in the camps. These individuals presumably have ties to ISIS, given that they have traveled to Syria to live in ISIS-controlled areas. They are often the family members of ISIS fighters and come primarily from Europe, North Africa, and Central Asia. However, it is important to note that these connections do not mean that they currently support ISIS. By all accounts, ISIS supporters in the camps remain a minority—but they are active and sometimes violent, possibly giving them an outsized influence on life in the foreigners' annex.

Unlike IDPs and refugees, these individuals—sometimes referred to as *detainees*—do not have specific protections under international law, and decisions about whether and how to repatriate them are at the discretion of their home countries. To date, their countries of origin have been reluctant to permit them to return home. The most-common reasons are political and security-related: Foreigners currently housed in the camps might be ISIS supporters or people who conducted atrocities for ISIS, but a lack of evidence to assess their activities or prosecute them at home would likely result in their release into their former communities. They might not be accepted, or—worst-case scenario—they could conduct an attack. Very few exceptions have been made, which were mostly in the case of children in dire need of medical treatment.

Political barriers to repatriation also extend to Syrians and Iraqis housed at the camps. Specifically, community leaders might be reluctant to sponsor returnees because of a widespread assumption among Syrian and Iraqi publics that those who remain in the camps have ties to ISIS— whether or not those concerns are valid. Other camp residents, particularly those in minority groups, might fear discrimination or violence upon returning home.

The lack of political will on the part of government officials has meant indefinite detention for those housed in the foreigners' annex. For children living in the camps, this translates to a lost childhood and, potentially, lost adulthood—making them vulnerable to the influence of ISIS and other extremist groups with an unclear degree of presence in the camps that could also pose a threat to the broader region.

In addition to supporting efforts to stabilize Iraq and Syria and to facilitate the return of all camp residents to their homes, there are steps that governments should take to establish clear legal procedures to repatriate their citizens:

- Develop a process to determine the legal status of foreigners in the camps.
- Develop and resource judicial systems in the AANES to investigate, collect evidence, and try suspected ISIS affiliates. This could be supported by a quantification of the scope of the problem and an independent assessment of patterns of radicalization within the camps and connections to external ISIS networks.
- Establish assessment structures and processes to determine safe paths for repatriating adolescent boys, who are most vulnerable to radicalization.

There is also a need to identify feasible paths to resettlement for those who cannot return to their homes because of discrimination, including a reassessment of asylum and refugee processes.

Overcrowding, unhygienic living conditions, limited access to services, and poor security pose a risk to the current and future well-being of camp residents. The Syrian Civil War and the counter-ISIS campaign have displaced millions of people in Syria and Iraq. Al-Hol, for example, was designed to hold a maximum of 40,000 people, but its population surged to 73,000 after the March 2019 liberation of Baghouz, the last sliver of territory held by ISIS in Syria. At both al-Hol and Roj, around two-thirds of residents are under the age of 18.

Given this overcrowding, humanitarian conditions at al-Hol are particularly dire; residents contend with insufficient facilities, overtaxed sewers, malnutrition, and a risk of disease outbreaks, including coronavirus disease 2019 (COVID-19) transmission. More than 450 children died at the camp in the months after the March 2019 population surge.

NGOs operate basic schools and health clinics at the camps, but limited resources and high demand make it difficult to access these services. Beyond the challenges of maintaining good physical health under poor sanitary conditions, displaced populations are often coping with the effects of trauma and require mental health services. A lack of support for emotional wellness could make residents more susceptible to radicalization and militarization. Compounding these problems is the fact that children previously educated in ISIS schools do not arrive at the camps with a solid educational foundation, given that the group banned certain subjects and used classrooms to promote its ideology. And the education that children receive in the camps is rudimentary—if they can access it at all. Only 40 percent of children in al-Hol and 88 percent of children in Roj attend NGO-run schools. The COVID-19 pandemic also led to temporary shutdowns, further limiting access to health care and education services. Inadequate sanitation, nutrition, and access to health care jeopardize the well-being of the camps' residents, while poor access to education could lead to long-term disadvantages for children who grow up in the camps.

A job provides a path to independence for working-age residents, but the camps' locations make it extremely difficult to travel to work. There are some occupational opportunities within the camps, but most roles are low-skilled. Although some residents have been able to launch their own business ventures or engage in the informal labor market, for others, the inability to leave the camp, make money, and support a family can exacerbate feelings of isolation.

The security situation is similarly problematic. Camps across the region have been attacked, violence has broken out between residents and guards, residents have been targeted by ISIS supporters, and human smugglers pose a threat to those who seek to leave. Although the extent of radicalization and ISIS affiliation in the camps is unclear, anecdotal evidence indicates that some former ISIS wives, and likely their children, are disillusioned and no longer support the group or its ideology. However, some women in the al-Hol foreigners' annex actively support ISIS goals and have attempted to establish governance and education systems in the group's style, spread ISIS propaganda, and violently attack those who do not adhere to its ideology. This presence of adherents poses a risk to other residents who are isolated in the foreigners' annex—particularly adolescent boys. It is possible that allowing those housed in the foreigners' annex to intermingle with the rest of the camp's population could dilute the influence of ISIS adherents.

Recommendations to improve conditions at the camps and better prepare residents to return to their communities lean heavily toward funding mechanisms and priorities:

- Increase funding and resources to improve housing conditions, sanitation, hygiene, access to clean water, and access to physical and mental health services.

- Increase funding to improve services at the camps and provide appropriate security support for the NGOs that deliver these services.
- Establish an international fund with mandatory contributions from nations with citizens who are currently housed in the camps.
- Increase the size of the security force and its funding, training, equipment, and other resources.
- Increase integration among camp residents and allow greater freedom of movement between the camps and local communities to provide economic opportunities to residents. Consider isolating only the most-radicalized foreigners, using an independent security assessment.

Laying the Foundation for Successful Repatriation

Repatriating and resettling the camps' residents—which would alleviate pressure on the AANES, SDF, and NGOs servicing the camps—has proceeded slowly and sporadically, largely because of home countries' lack of political will. Monitoring and preventing radicalization among camp residents and providing support to the AANES and SDF efforts to settle internally displaced Syrians in their home communities or in northeastern Syria will be critical. Diplomatic pressure, along with humanitarian and judicial assistance, will be necessary to assist the Iraqi government as it likewise confronts the challenge of bringing its citizens home.

The most difficult legal and policy challenges will be repatriating foreign families who currently lack legal protections and are being detained at the camps for indefinite periods. To assist in these efforts, the United States and allied countries should continue to apply diplomatic pressure to motivate repatriation and provide technical assistance as needed.

Until camp residents can return to their home communities or nations, it will be critical to ensure proper humanitarian and security conditions. At a minimum, we urge that the international community dedicate greater financial and physical resources to these camps to improve the quality of living conditions and medical and education services. Al-Hol and Roj also suffer from a limited security presence and oversight. A well-resourced security force can make a significant difference in the living conditions at the camps by supporting greater integration and reducing isolation for non-radicalized foreigners. Residents would benefit from as many opportunities as possible to resist radicalization and prepare them for repatriation and, ultimately, a new start.

Contents

Figures and Tables

Figures

Tables

CHAPTER ONE

Introduction

In March 2011, amid popular uprisings across the Middle East and North Africa, Syrians began peacefully protesting against the regime of President Bashar al-Assad. What began in Dar'a in southwestern Syria quickly expanded to Damascus, Aleppo, and other cities throughout the country. In the ensuing months, protests transitioned into an insurgency against the regime, which violently attempted to repress the demonstrations, ultimately escalating the situation into a civil war. Over the next few years, the al-Assad regime and its foreign allies focused most of their military efforts along the western spine of Syria, with limited attention on the eastern portion of the country, which is largely desert.[1] Subsequently, in early March 2013, the eastern city of ar-Raqqah became the first provincial capital captured by the opposition.[2] Fighting between the regime, Syrian opposition, and, ultimately, the Islamic State of Iraq and Syria (ISIS) continued across eastern Syria, often involving fratricidal clashes between anti-regime forces.[3] By late summer, ISIS was fighting both the opposition and the Syrian regime in eastern Syria and up to the Euphrates River in northern Syria. In January 2014, ISIS gained complete control of ar-Raqqah from rival elements of

---

[1] For a detailed timeline of events related to the Syrian Civil War, see Wilson Center, "Syria," webpage, undated.

[2] Nate Rosenblatt and David Kilcullen, *How Raqqa Became the Capital of ISIS*, Washington, D.C.: New America, July 2019.

[3] Eric Robinson, Daniel Egel, Patrick B. Johnston, Sean Mann, Alexander D. Rothenberg, and David Stebbins, *When the Islamic State Comes to Town: The Economic Impact of Islamic State Governance in Iraq and Syria*, Santa Monica, Calif.: RAND Corporation, RR-1970-RC, 2017; European Asylum Support Office, "Deir Ez-Zor," webpage, September 2020.

the opposition and proclaimed the city as its capital. ISIS would ultimately control a third of Syrian territory and establish governance, often through violence and repression, in its so-called caliphate.

Almost concurrently, the terrorist group Islamic State of Iraq was continuing its insurgent campaign against the Iraqi government, predominately in the country's Sunni-majority northern and western provinces. After launching military offensives in mid-2013—capturing multiple cities in the western al-Anbar Province—in early June 2014, the group began an operation against the northwestern city of Mosul. After a few weeks of fighting, Iraqi Security Forces were mostly fleeing, and ISIS's leader, Abu Bakr al-Baghdadi, announced the establishment of the group. He proclaimed himself the caliph, or the leader of the Muslim community, on June 29, 2014.[4] The United States began to conduct airstrikes against ISIS in Iraq by August, per the request of the Iraqi government.[5]

The United States, with support from members of the Global Coalition to Defeat ISIS, began military operations against ISIS in Syria in late September 2014. This air campaign coalesced around the town of Kobani to support the Syrian Kurdish People's Protection Units (YPG) fighting ISIS.[6] The YPG would become the backbone of the Syrian Democratic Forces (SDF), the ground force formed in late 2015 that partnered with U.S. and coalition forces to liberate ISIS-controlled areas of Syria. For the next five years, the SDF—with the support of coalition forces—advanced from northeastern Syria to liberate ar-Raqqah in October 2017. In March 2019, they eventually liberated the southeastern town of Baghouz—ISIS's last sliver of territory.[7]

The fight to liberate eastern Syria from ISIS caused widespread destruction and displacement; hundreds of thousands of Syrians were forced from

---

[4] "Video Claims to Show Islamic State Leader Abu Bakr al-Baghdadi Giving Sermon—Video," Reuters, July 6, 2014.

[5] For a detailed timeline of events related to the rise of ISIS in Iraq, see Wilson Center, "Timeline: The Rise, Spread, and Fall of the Islamic State," October 28, 2019.

[6] The Kurdish Project, "YPG: People's Protection Units," webpage, undated.

[7] Combined Joint Task Force–Operation Inherent Resolve, "Syrian Democratic Forces Liberate Raqqa," news release, U.S. Department of Defense, October 20, 2017; Rodi Said, "Islamic State 'Caliphate' Defeated, Yet Threat Persists," Reuters, March 23, 2019.

their homes.[8] The broader Syrian Civil War had displaced more than 13 million Syrians, more than half of whom were displaced internally within Syria's borders and living in camps, informal settlements, or urban areas.[9]

This report focuses on the displaced population currently residing in two prominent camps in northeastern Syria: al-Hol and Roj. Both camps host substantial foreign populations; many of the camps' residents lived under ISIS control for years, with some still promulgating the group's ideology. Their populations also include Iraqi refugees who fled ISIS control in northwestern Iraq. The nature of the camps—bringing together Iraqi refugees, Syrian internally displaced persons (IDPs), and third-country nationals—poses a unique challenge to efforts to decrease support for ISIS's ideology in the camps, one that became particularly acute with the influx of ISIS adherents after the fall of Baghouz. The presence of devoted ISIS followers in the camps could increase the risk of an ISIS resurgence in northeastern Syria as well.

Research Questions

The catalyst for this research was to understand the scenario of an already radicalized population becoming displaced and then living among civilians who sought to escape the repressive rule of ISIS in northeastern Syria and western Iraq. Thus, this report aims to shed light on the status of the presumed ISIS-radicalized element of displaced persons in the al-Hol and Roj camps and variables that could allow for the radicalization of other camp residents. Specifically, this research addresses the following questions:

- What is the disposition of inhabitants in the refugee and IDP camps at al-Hol and Roj?
- What human and security risks do these inhabitants face, and how could they contribute to radicalization in the camps?

---

[8]   Victor J. Blue, "After the 'War of Annihilation' Against ISIS," *Time*, April 6, 2019.

[9]   United Nations High Commissioner for Refugees (UNHCR), "Syria Emergency," webpage, March 15, 2021; Kathryn Reid, "Syrian Refugee Crisis: Facts, FAQs, and How to Help," World Vision, March 11, 2021.

- What lessons can be learned from historical cases, and could these lessons highlight potential policy solutions?

It is important to emphasize that refugees and displaced persons are not inherently more radicalized than the broader population. However, the particular circumstances of these camps—ISIS families mixed with displaced civilians and broader elements of isolation—might increase the vulnerability of the camps' residents to radicalization.

Refugees and Radicalization

Academic scholarship, along with the international community, lacks a single definition of the term *radicalization*. For this report, we define *radicalization* as a phased process through which an individual increasingly accepts the use of violence to achieve political, ideological, and/or religious goals that are often considered radical or threaten the status quo.[10] Moreover, simply holding radicalized views does not automatically mean that an individual will act upon them and conduct violence in support of achieving those goals.

Although displaced persons might be targeted for recruitment by armed groups or might choose to join militant groups, it does not appear that they join militant organizations at higher rates than the general population. Our study did not compare or have findings about overall recruitment of displaced people compared with the general public, but other work we reviewed has. For instance, Sadaf Lakhani and Rahmatullah Amiri focused on radicalization of displaced individuals in Afghanistan and found that displaced people were no more likely to militarize or radicalize than the general public.[11] In *Lessening the Risk of Refugee Radicalization*, Barbara

---

[10] Norwegian Ministry of Justice and Public Security, *Action Plan Against Radicalisation and Violent Extremism*, Oslo, August 28, 2014, p. 7; Directorate-General for Migration and Home Affairs, European Commission, "Prevention of Radicalisation," webpage, undated; Anja Dalgaard-Nielsen, "Violent Radicalization in Europe: What We Know and What We Do Not Know," *Studies in Conflict and Terrorism*, Vol. 33, No. 9, 2010, p. 798.

[11] Sadaf Lakhani and Rahmatullah Amiri, *Displacement and the Vulnerability to Mobilize for Violence: Evidence from Afghanistan*, Washington, D.C.: United States Institute of Peace, No. 155, January 2020.

Sude, David Stebbins, and Sarah Weilant found that radicalization and resulting armed militancy are not inevitable among refugees, even those in camps. Instead, a combination of factors—including access to economic opportunities, geographic location of camps, legal status of refugees, the actions of the receiving country, and the preexistence of militant groups in refugee areas—influence the likelihood of radicalization.[12]

Refugee and IDP camps are often infiltrated by armed groups, and the literature has identified residents of these camps as a target of armed group recruitment. Past research has similarly found that refugee and IDP camps can become militarized when the state allows, overlooks, or is unable to prevent camp penetration by armed groups—regardless of the numbers of members.[13] Some scholarship has argued that displacement in and of itself can perpetuate conflict because refugee and IDP camps can provide armed groups with a supply of recruits, especially if a group is open to or actively recruiting child soldiers.[14] Other studies have found that displaced people are more likely to be targeted if they are former members of an armed group (whether membership was forced is unimportant), if they have expressed economic frustrations about life in a camp, or if individuals in their network are members of an armed group.[15] However, as noted earlier, throughout this study of radicalism within displacement camps, we emphasize that refugees and displaced persons are not inherently more radicalized than the broader population. It is the particular circumstances of these camps, in

---

[12] Barbara Sude, David Stebbins, and Sarah Weilant, *Lessening the Risk of Refugee Radicalization: Lessons for the Middle East from Past Crises*, Santa Monica, Calif.: RAND Corporation, PE-166-OSD, 2015.

[13] Barbara H. Sude, "Prevention of Radicalization to Terrorism in Refugee Camps and Asylum Centers," in Alex P. Schmid, ed., *Handbook of Terrorism Prevention and Preparedness*, 1st ed., The Hague, the Netherlands: International Centre for Counter-Terrorism, 2020; Idean Salehyan, "Transnational Rebels: Neighboring States as Sanctuary for Rebel Groups," *World Politics,* Vol. 59, No. 2, 2007.

[14] Kelly E. Atkinson, "Refugees and Recruitment: Understanding Violations Against Children in Armed Conflict with Novel Data," *Journal of Peacebuilding and Development,* Vol. 15, No. 1, 2020.

[15] Roos Haer and Tobias Hecker, "Recruiting Refugees for Militarization: The Determinants of Mobilization Attempts," *Journal of Refugee Studies,* Vol. 32, No. 1, 2019.

which ISIS families are mixed with displaced civilians, that pose such risks and increase the vulnerability of the residents.

Approach and Limitations

We used three primary methods to address the questions that drove this research. First, we reviewed relevant literature that included journal articles, government and think tank reports, and press articles to develop a picture of the humanitarian situation and the presence and reach of ISIS in the camps.

Second, we complemented this research with 14 interviews with officials from the U.S. government, representatives of human rights and refugee support organizations, and Autonomous Administration of North and East Syria (AANES) officials to receive the most-updated information about the situation in the camps and their understanding of the presence and activity of ISIS in the camps. Our not-for-attribution interviews were conducted in late 2020 and early 2021. Any status updates came from press articles and think tank reports but reflect the status of the camps and northeastern Syria in summer 2021, not beyond.

Third, we explored more broadly the factors for radicalization and variables among refugee and displaced populations that might contribute to increased rates of militancy. Building on existing RAND research, we compiled a collection of cases from the past 30 years looking at newly displaced populations and multigenerationally displaced people to identify similarities and differences with northeastern Syria. We selected our cases from populations of displaced people from Afghanistan, Algeria, Burma, Palestine, Rwanda, Somalia, South Sudan, Sri Lanka, Western Sahara, and Yemen.

In the process of conducting this research, we faced a few limitations. First, because of the coronavirus disease 2019 (COVID-19) pandemic, we were unable to travel to the camps. However, our interviews with AANES officials and human rights and refugee support organizations, in particular, provided insight into the situation in the camps. Second, the scope of this work did not permit us to conduct individual interviews or focus groups with camp residents, which prevented an assessment of the full scope of ISIS membership and influence. This would be an important future research step.

Road Map to This Report

This report begins in Chapter Two by laying out policy challenges and considerations for the AANES, the United States and the Global Coalition to Defeat ISIS, and the broader international community regarding the situation in northeastern Syrian camps. Camp residents are a mix of IDPs and refugees, but some are also referred to as *detainees* (often Westerners who came to fight for and live in the so-called caliphate). The ambiguity of foreigners' legal status leads to questions about how they can return home, the broader security concerns they pose, and what legal processes exist to ensure fair justice.

Chapter Three examines the current status of the displaced persons camps under the jurisdiction of the AANES, a predominantly Kurdish non-state actor, in collaboration with multiple international nongovernmental organizations (NGOs), including the United Nations. The chapter also provides overviews of the history of al-Hol and Roj, the services provided there, the demographics of camp inhabitants, and the presence of ISIS. The humanitarian crisis affecting refugees and displaced populations in northwestern Syria remains critical, but we opted to focus on the myriad humanitarian and policy challenges resulting from the conflict to combat ISIS in the northeastern part of the country. Chapter Four highlights the humanitarian challenges faced by camp inhabitants, including public health limitations and the lack of education and economic opportunities. Chapter Five explores the security risks present in the camps, including the extent to which presumed ISIS members remain radicalized, their ability to propagate the ISIS ideology and lifestyle within the camps, connections with ISIS members not living in the camps, and the level of disillusionment among presumed ISIS members who might no longer view themselves as supporters of the group or believers of its ideology. Chapter Six presents our conclusions and recommendations.

CHAPTER TWO

Legal Definitions and Processes

Prior to a discussion of the inadequate humanitarian conditions and poor security environment of refugee and IDP camps in northeastern Syria, it is useful to briefly explore some relevant legal and policy challenges. Camp residents face a complex policy landscape in terms of their legal status and unclear right to return to their countries and communities of origin. A lack of control over these factors increases their vulnerability. Iraqis and Syrians in the camps face a potential return to areas that remain mired in violent conflict or that are rebuilding from the counter-ISIS campaign or the Syrian Civil War; therefore, remaining in al-Hol or Roj might be the safest option for them. However, Western countries with citizens in al-Hol often refuse to repatriate their nationals or resolve questions relating to citizenship, deradicalization, and repatriation, de facto consigning women and children to an extended life in the camps. Officials from Western countries might believe that they are avoiding potential threats from individuals with perceived ISIS affiliations, but in the long term, the risk of *not* addressing the living situation in the camps could increase camp residents' vulnerability and promote radicalization and living conditions that are unacceptable if they are long-term, potentially perpetuating a source of support for ISIS.

Who Lives in the Northeastern Syria Refugee and Internally Displaced Persons Camps?

There are three broad categories of residents at al-Hol and Roj, each of which has a different recognized or protected legal status. First, there are Syrian IDPs fleeing ISIS rule in eastern Syria and fleeing the fighting in western Syria from the broader Syrian Civil War. This group could also include ISIS-affiliated people. Second, there are Iraqi refugees, many of whom came to al-Hol after fleeing the counter-ISIS campaign in Iraq. However, ISIS supporters are almost certainly a part of al-Hol's Iraqi population, and many communities in Iraq consider the Iraqis in al-Hol—writ large—to be ISIS affiliates.[1] The final group consists of foreigners from outside the region, mostly Europe, North Africa, and Central Asia. These individuals presumably have ties to ISIS, given that they traveled to Syria to live in ISIS-controlled areas. These are mainly women, most of whom had been married to ISIS fighters, and their children. However, their status as foreigners does not necessarily correspond to current, active support for the group. Table 2.1 shows the estimated population of each group at the al-Hol and Roj camps. Some proportion of residents have become disillusioned with ISIS and disavowed the group.

Both refugees and IDPs are internationally recognized categories with legal protections, but this is not necessarily the case for this third group. The United Nations defines *refugees* and *IDPs* as follows:

- A *refugee* is "a person who is outside his/her country of nationality or habitual residence; has a well-founded fear of persecution because of his/her race, religion, nationality, membership in a particular social group or political opinion; and is unable or unwilling to avail himself/herself of the protection of that country, or to return there, for fear of persecution."[2]
- *IDPs* are "persons or groups of persons who have been forced or obliged to flee or to leave their homes or places of habitual residence, in particular as a result of or in order to avoid the effects of armed conflict, situations of generalized violence, violations of human rights or natural or

---

[1] Sarhang Hamasaeed, "What Will Become of Iraqis in Al-Hol?" United States Institute of Peace, November 19, 2020; Sam Mednick, "Inside the Troubled Repatriation of Iraqis from Syria's Al-Hol Camp," *New Humanitarian*, June 7, 2021.

[2] United Nations, "Definition of the Term 'Refugee,'" Article 1A(2), in United Nations High Commissioner for Refugees, *Convention and Protocol Relating to the Status of Refugees*, Geneva, Switzerland, [1951] 2010, p. 14.

TABLE 2.1

Categories of Inhabitants in the al-Hol and Roj Displacement Camps

Country of Origin	Category	Estimated Presence
Syria	IDPs or detainees	20,600[a]
Iraq	Refugees or detainees	30,800
Foreign countries[b]	Undetermined	11,100

[a] The estimated 20,600 Syrian IDPs include Syrians at al-Hol and Roj only. There are approximately 700,000 displaced Syrians in the country's Kurdish-controlled areas, so an estimate of all Syrian IDPs in Kurdish-controlled camps would likely be higher by an order of magnitude.

[b] The contingent of foreign families in al-Hol represents more than 60 different countries, and citizens of each country face a different repatriation process.

human-made disasters, and who have not crossed an internationally recognized border."[3]

- *Detainees* are "persons who have been subject to custodial deprivation of their liberty."[4]

The International Committee of the Red Cross (ICRC) defines *detention* as "the deprivation of liberty caused by the act of confining a person in a narrowly bounded place, under the control or with the consent of a State, or, in non-international armed conflicts, a non-State actor. Detainees cannot exercise many of their freedoms, including that of leaving the place of detention at will."[5] The ICRC has not stated whether foreign families living in the camps are "detained"; legal thresholds have not been established in international humanitarian law or international human rights law.[6]

---

[3] United Nations Economic and Social Council, "Introduction: Scope and Purpose, Paragraph 2," in *Guiding Principles on Internal Displacement*, February 11, 1998, p. 5.

[4] International Committee of the Red Cross, "Detainees," webpage, undated a.

[5] International Committee of the Red Cross, "Detention," webpage, undated b.

[6] Of note, the detention discussion extends beyond the foreigners in al-Hol and Roj. The AANES and SDF have employed methods and practices to ensure security in and around al-Hol and Roj, including restricting freedom of movement for all camp inhabitants. Moreover, questions regarding freedom of movement of refugees and IDPs emerge from camps in other countries. International law provides guidelines when detention of refugees is "reasonable and proportionate to a legitimate purpose." Refugees and dis-

The U.S. Department of Defense (DoD), U.S. Department of State (DoS), and the U.S. Agency for International Development Lead Inspector General note,

> The DIA [Defense Intelligence Agency] and the International Crisis Group report described women in the foreign annex as detainees, held in separate areas of Al Hol and other camps along with their children. USAID [the U.S. Agency for International Development], the DoS, and the OUSD(P)/ISA [Office of the Under Secretary of Defense (Policy)/ International Security Affairs] stated that women and their children in the foreign annex of Al Hol are not detained, and should not be referred to as "detainees." However, open source reporting indicates that the residents of the annex are under guard. USAID reported last quarter that residents of the annex must be escorted when going to the market in the camp.[7]

Others have argued that al-Hol and Roj's foreign residents are undeniably detainees, given the restrictions on their movement and the constant presence of security guards.[8] Some NGO officials and researchers specifically refer to the foreigners as *detainees*, given the restrictions of their movements and inability to leave the camp freely, noting that the difference in language affects the types of services that aid groups can provide in the camps.[9] This report only highlights the variations in how this group of camp inhabitants

---

placed persons might generally be detained as "necessary" by countries of refuge while their claims are being processed, for example. Moreover, maintenance of security—to include checkpoints, security screening, and internment—is also considered a "reasonable" basis for detention. See United Nations, "Refugees Unlawfully in the Country of Refugee," Article 31(2), in United Nations High Commissioner for Refugees, *Convention and Protocol Relating to the Status of Refugees*, Geneva, Switzerland, [1951] 2010, p. 29.

[7] U.S. Department of Defense, Office of Inspector General, *Operation Inherent Resolve: Lead Inspector General Report to the United States Congress*, Alexandria, Va., October 1, 2019–December 31, 2019b, p. 48.

[8] Rights and Security International, *Europe's Guantanamo: The Indefinite Detention of European Women and Children in North East Syria*, Version 2, London, February 17, 2021, p. 16.

[9] Interview with NGO workers, phone, November 25, 2020; interview with an NGO worker, phone, January 14, 2021.

are referred to and does not provide a determination of their legal status. In light of this complexity, we refer to this category of people as *foreigners* or *foreign families*, without addressing the legal discussion surrounding *detention*.

Women and children in the foreigners' annex of the camps could also face increased challenges in obtaining sufficient health services and other humanitarian aid. According to the International Crisis Group, "the ambiguity of women's and children's legal status (they are neither formally displaced persons, nor prisoners, nor conflict detainees) has slowed the delivery of services a refugee or internally displaced persons camp would normally receive."[10] This ambiguity also has complicated efforts to repatriate individuals who wish to return home when their home countries deny their request to return. The scope of this research permitted only a cursory examination of these categories of camp residents; further legal analysis is required to appropriately address the nuances of each category. Ultimately, we determined that the presence of all these groups, at al-Hol, in particular—coupled with the perception of ISIS affiliation—presented challenges in providing services to the camps.

Repatriation and Reconciliation Processes and Challenges

The repatriation of foreigners, refugees, and IDPs or their reconciliation with their home communities present enormous challenges. These include

- **the unique status of different groups.** The repatriation of foreigners, refugees, and IDPs or their reconciliation with their home communities present enormous challenges that differ with the status of these groups. Moreover, even within the broad categories we have identified, there are nuances. For example, there are certainly ISIS members and supporters within the Syrian and Iraqi populations, and they should face appropriate judicial proceedings. However, efforts to determine the appropriate category for inhabitants are slow and underfunded.

---

[10] International Crisis Group, *Women and Children First: Repatriating the Westerners Affiliated with ISIS*, Middle East Report No. 208, Brussels, November 18, 2019, p. 4.

- **working with the AANES as counterpart**. Adding to the political and bureaucratic difficulties, the AANES itself has a complicated legal status because it is not an internationally recognized state. In fact, because the Syrian government led by Bashar al-Assad remains internationally recognized, much-needed international aid and support often faces additional hurdles. Yet, it should be noted that the AANES still has to observe international humanitarian law to protect refugees, IDPs, and detainees under its control.[11]

- **definitional ambiguity**. Whether the camp inhabitants are refugees or detainees has significant implications for their rights and future. Of particular interest is adherence to the 1951 Refugee Convention, which upholds the principle of *non-refoulement*, meaning that it is illegal to force individuals to return to a country where they could "face torture, cruel, inhuman, or degrading treatment or punishment or other irreparable harm."[12] This principle is generally applied to discussions about Iraqis in al-Hol who cannot be forced to return home. Many in Iraq consider those still living in camps (whether in Syria or Iraq) to be affiliated with ISIS, leading to societal exclusion. Although some Iraqis in the camps might indeed be ISIS-affiliated, there are insufficient judicial procedures to determine previous or current support for the group. However, if an individual is determined to be ISIS-affiliated, non-refoulement protections do not apply.

- **inconsistent policies of stakeholder governments**. As discussed earlier, the legal status of foreigners with perceived ISIS connections remains a complicated legal and policy question, which each foreign country has dealt with differently. Some countries have repatriated their citizens, who subsequently face domestic justice systems. Other countries— particularly those in western Europe—have only sparingly repatriated their nationals, for a variety of domestic political reasons. This report

---

[11] Jonathan Horowitz, "Kurdish-Held Detainees in Syria Are Not in a 'Legal Gray Area,'" *Just Security*, April 13, 2018; International Committee of the Red Cross, *Internally Displaced Persons and International Humanitarian Law*, Geneva, Switzerland, December 2017.

[12] Office of the United Nations High Commissioner for Human Rights, "The Principle of *Non-Refoulement* Under International Human Rights Law," undated.

does not delve into the reasons for those decisions except to note that there are policy and ethical questions about the implications of allowing people to live in the camps indefinitely under undetermined legal status.

In the next sections, we discuss the broad categories of camp inhabitants (foreigners, Syrians, and Iraqis) and highlight some of the unique challenges each face.

Foreigners

Since the wave of displaced persons entered al-Hol in 2019, Kurdish regional authorities, the U.S. government, NGOs, and researchers have urged the international community to repatriate their nationals from the camps, especially the approximately 1,500 foreign children in al-Hol and Roj. Some countries have been more willing than others to accept their nationals who traveled to Syria to join ISIS. The United States and former Soviet Union states—such as Russia, Kazakhstan, and Uzbekistan—have led the way in repatriating their nationals. Malaysia and Indonesia have also been proactive in doing so.[13]

However, many other countries have remained reluctant to repatriate women and children from al-Hol, Roj, and, at least until October 2019, Ain Issa. Researchers and activists have been particularly critical of such Western countries as Canada, France, and the United Kingdom for their reluctance to repatriate their nationals except in extreme circumstances. For instance, when a seven-year-old girl French girl in al-Hol required lifesaving medical treatment, the French government had a medical plane return her to Paris; however, her mother, three siblings, and around 300 other children of French origin were required to remain in Syria.[14] Canada repatriated a five-year-old girl who was orphaned in Syria when her parents and siblings

---

[13] Aaron Y. Zelin, *Wilayat al-Hawl: "Remaining" and Incubating the Next Islamic State Generation*, Washington, D.C.: Washington Institute for Near East Policy, PN70, October 2019, p. 10; International Crisis Group, 2019; Lila Hassan, "Repatriating ISIS Foreign Fighters Is Key to Stemming Radicalization, Experts Say, but Many Countries Don't Want Their Citizens Back," *Frontline*, April 6, 2021.

[14] Ben Hubbard and Constant Méheut, "Western Countries Leave Children of ISIS in Syrian Camps," *New York Times*, May 31, 2020.

were killed in the final stages of the counter-ISIS campaign in 2019; however, Canadian Prime Minister Justin Trudeau affirmed that the girl's case was "exceptional" because she was the only Canadian orphan in Syria. The Canadian government took no action to repatriate its remaining citizens in AANES and SDF custody—25 children, 13 women, and eight men.[15]

Many of the countries that have heretofore refused to fully repatriate their nationals have given legal and political reasons for their decisions. Some European governments argue that their terrorism laws would not allow them to prosecute many of the women who traveled to Syria because of a lack of evidence tying the women to formal ISIS membership or participation in acts of terrorism. Even when countries could gather sufficient evidence to prosecute a case, terrorism laws might only provide for limited sentences of a few years, after which potentially ISIS-affiliated individuals could be back on the streets in their countries of origin.[16] Should they then revert back to supporting the group or another Salafi-Jihadi organization or—in a worst-case scenario—conduct an attack on their home soil, the political blowback would likely be enormous for government officials who allowed the repatriation. Therefore, many governments have opted to delay decisions and let their nationals remain in Syria, and continue relying on the SDF and Asayesh officials to guard them in al-Hol and Roj.[17]

Several experts and officials interviewed for this study emphasized the need to repatriate foreigners in al-Hol and Roj to their countries of origin. In particular and at minimum, they advocated repatriating those who were children when their parents brought them to Syria or the small children who might have been born in the ISIS caliphate. They emphasized that children are considered victims under international humanitarian law and, there-

---

[15] Letta Tayler, "Don't Let Orphan's Canadian Homecoming Be an Exception," Human Rights Watch, October 6, 2020.

[16] However, the AANES also lacks appropriate judicial systems to collect evidence, hold, and try suspected former and current ISIS members for crimes. See Hassan, 2021; Nadim Houry, "Bringing ISIS to Justice: Running Out of Time?" Human Rights Watch, February 5, 2019.

[17] For a more comprehensive discussion of the options for repatriation and legal hurdles and considerations, see Brian Michael Jenkins, "Options for Dealing with Islamic State Foreign Fighters Currently Detained in Syria," *CTC Sentinel*, Vol. 12, No. 5, May–June 2019, p. 17; Rights and Security International, 2021; International Crisis Group, 2019.

fore, should not be condemned for their parents' crimes.[18] Although this option could prevent children's lost childhoods from turning into lost adulthoods, multiple barriers remain. Separating children from their parents is illegal under international human rights law, international humanitarian law, and international refugee law.[19] In the case of the orphans, countries would face challenges of determining who would raise them. Moreover, processes do not yet exist to assess and treat potentially radicalized youth who have spent years living under ISIS influence and who could also be psychologically traumatized by their experiences.

Syrians

Returning Syrian IDPs to their communities of origin has been more successful than efforts to repatriate third-party nationals. Since the final campaigns against ISIS brought a wave of refugees, IDPs, and foreigners into al-Hol, the AANES and SDF have worked with the Syrian community and tribal leaders to resettle Syrian civilians in their places of origin. Through this process, AANES and SDF officials vet Syrian IDPs for ties to ISIS and past ISIS-related activities. In the absence of evidence tying them to the group, Syrian IDPs' return is sponsored by tribal leaders who vouch for Syrian IDPs' good conduct. The tribal sponsorship process led to a steady stream of departures of Syrian IDPs from camps in AANES territory, including more than 8,500 from al-Hol by early 2021.[20]

---

[18] Interview with a think tank researcher, Washington, D.C., November 11, 2020; interview with an academic, phone, November 12, 2020; interview with NGO workers, phone, November 25, 2020; interview with a think tank researcher, phone, December 4, 2020; interview with an NGO worker, phone, January 4, 2021.

[19] Frances Nicholson, *The Right to Family Life and Family Unity of Refugees and Others in Need of International Protection and the Family Definition Applied*, 2nd ed., Geneva, Switzerland: United Nations High Commissioner for Refugees, January 2018.

[20] Syrian IDPs in these camps also fled from regime- and Turkish-controlled areas of the country. Their ability to return home is important but beyond the scope of this research. See U.S. Department of Defense, Office of Inspector General, *Operation Inherent Resolve: Lead Inspector General Report to the United States Congress*, Alexandria, Va., January 1, 2021–March 31, 2021a, p. 75; Sofia Barbarani, "Leaving Syria's Notorious al-Hol Camp, Civilians Find Little to Go Home to," *New Humanitarian*, January 14, 2021.

However, on October 5, 2020, the AANES announced that it would expedite its efforts to return all Syrian IDPs to their communities of origin and would no longer require tribal leaders to sponsor the individuals' return. Instead, Kurdish security forces would conduct background checks and targeted—as opposed to comprehensive—interviews to determine the level of security risk these individuals pose before releasing them from the camps. The DoD Office of Inspector General (OIG) reported that the SDF released more than 1,600 Syrians from al-Hol in the last three months of 2020.[21]

Iraqis

The situation concerning al-Hol's Iraqi residents is also politically fraught, and there are barriers to repatriating them. In addition to the Iraqi refugees at al-Hol, the Iraqi government is struggling with its own internally displaced population as a result of the counter-ISIS campaign, which we discuss in Chapter Three. At the onset of the displacement crisis in northeastern Syria, Baghdad indicated that it would repatriate all its nationals who were residing in Syrian refugee and IDP camps, moving them to a special detention camp in Iraq.[22] However, the prospect of relocating more than 31,200 Iraqis with either real or perceived ties to ISIS spurred political resistance from Iraqi communities that did not want a detention camp near their homes. In particular, Iraqi government efforts to build a facility near Zumar in Ninewa Province met significant opposition from local activists

---

[21] U.S. Department of Defense, Office of Inspector General, *Operation Inherent Resolve: Lead Inspector General Report to the United States Congress*, Alexandria, Va., October 1, 2020–December 31, 2020c, p. 68.

[22] Louisa Loveluck and Mustafa Salim, "Iraq Is Pushing to Build an Isolation Camp for 30,000 Iraqis Who Lived Under ISIS in Syria," *Washington Post*, May 2, 2019. In its fiscal year (FY) 2019 third quarter report and at the height of the humanitarian crisis in al-Hol, OIG reported that the Iraqi government intended to repatriate all Iraqis in al-Hol within months; however, as detailed in the OIG report, the Iraqi government has continued to forestall moving its nationals from al-Hol to detention and processing centers in Iraq. See U.S. Department of Defense, Office of Inspector General, *Operation Inherent Resolve: Lead Inspector General Report to the United States Congress*, Alexandria, Va., April 1, 2019–June 30, 2019a, p. 5.

and politicians, at least temporarily halting the camp's construction and the repatriation process.[23]

Of note, Iraqis in al-Hol represent both sides of the conflict; they include civilians displaced by ISIS and the families of ISIS fighters. Following the removal of ISIS from the surrounding area in 2016, al-Hol was reopened, and thousands of Syrians and Iraqi refugees arrived at the camp to escape the violence and life in the so-called caliphate.[24] Families of Iraqi ISIS fighters also arrived following the fall of Baghouz in 2019.[25] This situation complicates efforts to determine the disposition of Iraqis in the camp and often leads to the broad and misplaced characterization of all Iraqis remaining in al-Hol as "ISIS-affiliated."

A steady trickle of Iraqis has departed al-Hol, sometimes reaching the Iraq border with the assistance of smugglers. When they turn themselves in to the Iraqi Security Forces, they are assessed to determine whether they pose a security risk. If they are cleared to continue, they can return to their places of origin with sponsorship from their local community leader. However, the longer the displaced Iraqi community remains in al-Hol, the more stigmatized they might become among the broader Iraqi populace. Public opinion might be that those who were *not* ISIS affiliates and wanted to return to Iraq would have done so already, and those still in al-Hol remain there because of their affinity for ISIS.[26] In reality, some 8,000 women and children have signaled their desire to return to Iraq; at the same time, many

---

[23] Interview with an Iraqi academic, phone, November 23, 2020; Ammar Aziz, "Work to Build Umla Camp for 'ISIS Families' Resumed," *Kirkuk Now*, October 22, 2020.

[24] Al-Hol was first established to accommodate Iraqi refugees from the 1991 Gulf War. It was reopened following Operation Iraqi Freedom in 2003. The camp closed in 2013 because of the Syrian Civil War and the rise of ISIS influence in the area. See Syrians for Truth and Justice, *Deaths in al-Hawl Refugee Camp After the Outbreak of Typhoid*, Strasbourg, France, May 2018; UNHCR, "Flash Update: Iraqi Refugee Response in Hassakeh, Syria 18–25 October 2016," October 26, 2016b; Monica Awad, "Iraqi Families Flee Mosul, Seeking Refuge Across the Syrian Border," UNICEF, November 7, 2016.

[25] Elizabeth Tsurkov, "Uncertainty, Violence, and the Fear of Fostering Extremism in Syria's al-Hol Camp," *New Humanitarian*, August 27, 2019.

[26] U.S. Department of Defense, Office of Inspector General, 2020c, pp. 68–69.

Iraqis in al-Hol fear repatriation and possible reprisals from both the Iraqi government and local communities because of their perceived ties to ISIS.[27]

Despite an apparent initial willingness in 2019 to repatriate its nationals from al-Hol, the Iraqi government continued to delay action on the issue at least until after the June 2021 parliamentary elections. Then–Prime Minister Mustafa al-Kadhimi's government showed reluctance to repatriate Iraqi nationals displaced in Syria. As one interviewee put it, "No one in the Iraqi government wants to be labeled with permitting the floodgates to open for ISIS-affiliated Iraqis," fearing political fallout and the impact that such a move might have at the polls.[28] Nevertheless, the SDF and the AANES have continued to push for Iraq to repatriate its nationals, particularly the thousands of Iraqi families residing in al-Hol before the March 2019 influx of displaced persons out of Baghouz.[29] AANES and SDF officials argue that these Iraqi families are not affiliated with ISIS and do not pose a security risk.[30] However, the Iraqi government reportedly considers the majority of the al-Hol Iraqi population to be ISIS affiliates,[31] which leads to questions about how returning Iraqis would be treated by the Iraqi government and the communities they return to. The Iraqi government has been slow to develop a plan to vet Iraqis displaced in Syria, determine whether they have ties to ISIS, and establish a system to legally process them upon their

---

[27] Hamasaeed, 2020.

[28] Interview with a U.S. government official, phone, December 2, 2020.

[29] Between May 2021 and October 2022, the Government of Iraq repatriated over 3,000 Iraqis from al-Hol. However, in November 2022, Prime Minister Mohammed Shia al-Sudani's government halted repatriations until a "new mechanism" could be developed. See Shelly Kittleson, "Iraq Suspends Repatriations from Syria's Notorious Islamic State Camp al-Hol," *Al-Monitor*, November 8, 2022; "Hundreds Linked to IS Transferred from Syria to Iraq," *Defense Post*, October 19, 2022; C. Todd Lopez, "DoD to Fund Better Detention Facilities in Syria, But Best Solution Is Detainee Repatriation," DoD News, July 14, 2022.

[30] As of late May 2021, 100 Iraqi families living in al-Hol were repatriated to a camp in Iraq's Ninewa Governorate after months of negotiations. Local Iraqis expressed serious concerns about the new camp's poor security and the return of the families. See Farid Abdul-Wahid and Samya Kullab, "100 Iraqi Families from IS-Linked Camp in Syria Repatriated," *Washington Post*, May 25, 2021.

[31] Interview with an Iraqi academic, phone, November 23, 2020.

eventual return to Iraq, continuing to postpone action despite al-Hol being a "looming disaster."[32]

Summary

In northeastern Syria, legal challenges compound the humanitarian and security situation in the camps. The ambiguous legal status of foreigners, in particular, and perceptions that those Syrians and Iraqis still living in the camps are affiliated with ISIS have overshadowed moral obligations to refugees and displaced persons. **The United States, the Global Coalition to Defeat ISIS, the European Union, and the United Nations should work with the AANES and appropriate NGOs to establish justice systems to determine the legal status of the foreigners remaining in al-Hol and Roj to facilitate their return to their home countries.** Previous RAND research found that in addition to the presence of armed groups in the camps, government policy decisions—or lack thereof—have contributed the most to the radicalization of displaced populations.[33] In particular, local and foreign government policies restricting freedom of movement, the right to return home, and economic agency can contribute to heightened rates of radicalization among displaced populations. **Additional resources and expertise should be provided to the AANES and SDF to increase security in and around the camps, along with best practices to limit freedom of movement and the resultant isolation of the camp inhabitants from economic opportunities.** Again, it is important to emphasize that the existence of such factors does not mean that all or even many displaced persons will be radicalized. Although each factor individually might not increase the potential that an individual—displaced or not—will radicalize, exposure to multiple such factors over time might increase the vulnerability of these populations to extremist groups and radicalization.

---

[32] Interview with a U.S. government official, December 11, 2020; interview with an Iraqi academic, phone, November 23, 2020.

[33] Sude, Stebbins, and Weilant, 2015.

CHAPTER THREE

Overview of Refugee and Internally Displaced Persons Camps in Northeastern Syria

The Syrian Civil War has resulted in hardships and human suffering. In addition to the approximately 228,000 noncombatants and 250,000 combatants killed in the conflict, 13 million Syrians—more than half of the country's prewar population—have fled their homes, with approximately 6.2 million Syrians displaced inside the country.[1] Syria's displacement crisis has touched every part of the country, yet Kurdish-controlled northeastern Syria is grappling with a unique set of challenges. In addition to the displaced Syrians, AANES and SDF officials, their international backers, and aid organizations are also contending with more than 9,000 foreign women and children displaced from ISIS's last Syrian holdouts, along with more than 30,000 Iraqi nationals. This chapter provides background of the major camps in northeastern Syria, a snapshot of their demographics, and a discussion of ISIS presence.

Background of Major Camps in Northeastern Syria

The 2015–2019 U.S.-backed military campaign to liberate ISIS-controlled areas in northeastern Syria led to large-scale population displacement, with civilians flooding Syrian IDP and refugee camps at Ain Issa, al-Hol, and

---

[1] Suleiman Al-Khalidi, "The Cost of Ten Years of Devastating War in Syria," Reuters, May 26, 2021; Médecins Sans Frontières, "A Decade of War in Syria: 10 Years of Increasing Humanitarian Needs," March 3, 2021.

Roj. In the latter half of 2020 alone, an estimated 700,000 individuals across the Kurdish-controlled areas remained displaced by the conflict.[2]

The camps are supervised by the Kurdish-led AANES, also known as the Self-Administration of North and East Syria. Blumont, in coordination with the UNHCR, provides camp coordination and camp management services. A variety of international NGOs provide humanitarian services to the camps. The AANES, through the SDF, provides security. Both organizations received significant support from the Global Coalition to Defeat ISIS, primarily to territorially defeat the group in northeastern Syria. After the fall of Baghouz, the coalition and the United States (through DoD and DoS) have provided limited funds to the AANES and SDF to support the administration and security of the camps. Figure 3.1 shows the locations of

FIGURE 3.1

Map of Primary Refugee Camps in Northeastern Syria

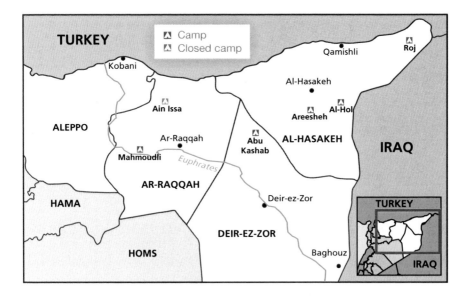

---

[2] Turkey's military incursion into northeastern Syria in October 2019 displaced, at least temporarily, an additional 200,000 people in the Hasakeh, Ar-Raqqah, and Aleppo provinces. See United Nations Office for the Coordination of Humanitarian Affairs, 2019b; Médecins Sans Frontières, 2020.

the primary refugee camps in northeastern Syria, and Table 3.1 provides the approximate number of inhabitants in the al-Hol and Roj camps.

Al-Hol Camp

The al-Hol camp, located 10 kilometers from the Iraq border and 40 kilometers from Hasakeh City, has experienced a significant increase in occupants. The camp was designed to hold a maximum of 40,000 people, but its population surged from 10,000 to 73,000 following the March 2019 liberation of Baghouz, the last sliver of territory held by ISIS.[3] The vast majority of camp residents—possibly up to 94 percent—are women and children, including the family members of ISIS fighters. After the fall of Baghouz, 11,000 women and children from more than 60 countries arrived at the camp and were isolated in a foreigners' annex that remains cordoned off from the Syrian and Iraqi populations.[4] Estimates suggest that, as of mid-2019, 67 percent of camp residents (approximately 49,000 people) were under the age of 18, with 20,000 residents who were under the age of five and born within the borders

TABLE 3.1

Approximate Number of Inhabitants in the al-Hol and Roj Displacement Camps

Camp	Category	Estimated Presence, as of June 2021
Al-Hol	• Syrians	20,400
	• Iraqis	30,600
	• Foreigners	9,000
	Total	**60,000**
Roj	• Syrians and Iraqis	400
	• Foreigners	2,100
	Total	**2,500**

SOURCE: U.S. Department of Defense, Office of Inspector General, *Operation Inherent Resolve: Lead Inspector General Report to the United States Congress*, Alexandria, Va., April 1, 2021–June 30, 2021b, pp. 18, 80.

NOTE: Approximately two thirds of residents in both al-Hol and Roj are children (approximately 40,200 and approximately 1,675, respectively). All data used for this report were current as of June 2021 and were not updated prior to the release of the report.

---

[3] Rights and Security International, 2021, p. 12.

[4] Zelin, 2019, p. 3; Julia C. Hurley, "Coronavirus and ISIS: The Challenge of Repatriation from Al-Hol," United States Institute of Peace, May 28, 2020.

of the so-called ISIS caliphate. Many children came to the camp unaccompanied by parents or guardians.[5] By the end of 2020, al-Hol's population had decreased to approximately 66,900 total residents, comprising 25,700 Syrians, 31,200 Iraqis, and 10,000 foreigners.[6] By the end of June 2021, al-Hol's population was just under 60,000 inhabitants, with Syrians at 34 percent (approximately 20,400), Iraqis at 51 percent (approximately 30,600), and foreigners at 15 percent (approximately 9,000).[7] More than two thirds of camp residents are children, and 50 percent of them are under the age of 12 (approximately 20,100).

Al-Hol provides a variety of services to camp residents, although service providers are stressed because of the size of the camp and security concerns (see Figure 3.2). To address the health needs of the camp's population, al-Hol has three makeshift hospitals and 23 clinics operated by international NGOs, such as Médecins Sans Frontières (Doctors Without Borders), ICRC, and the Kurdish Red Crescent. However, these facilities suffer from an insufficient number of doctors, pharmacists, and medical staff.[8] According to AANES officials interviewed for this study, NGOs operated 14 makeshift schools in al-Hol as of late 2020.[9]

Roj Camp

The Roj camp outside Qamishli in the far northeast corner of Syria holds the second-largest group of foreigners after al-Hol. As of early 2021, around 1,200 of the camp's total 1,800 residents were foreigners, and, similar to al-Hol, approximately two-thirds of the camp's population were under the age of 18.[10] To alleviate pressure on limited security bandwidth and services

---

[5] U.S. Department of Defense, Office of Inspector General, 2019a, p. 39.

[6] Interview with a Syrian Democratic Council official, phone, December 21, 2020.

[7] U.S. Department of Defense, Office of Inspector General, 2021b, p. 80.

[8] U.S. Department of Defense, Office of Inspector General, 2019a, p. 8; interview with a Syrian Democratic Council official, phone, December 21, 2020.

[9] Interview with a Kurdish official, phone, December 21, 2020; REACH, "Camp Profile: Al Hol," fact sheet, October 2020d.

[10] Rights and Security International, 2021, p. 12; REACH, "Camp Profile: Roj," fact sheet, October 2020e.

FIGURE 3.2
Map of al-Hol Camp

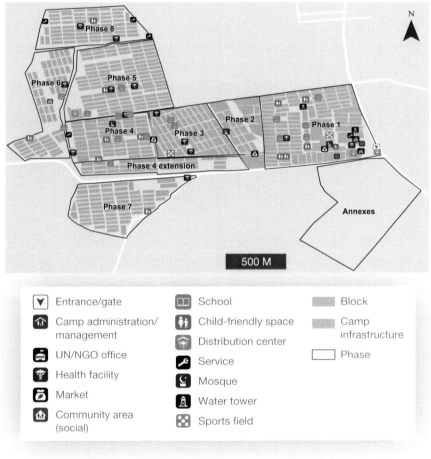

N

Phase 8
Phase 6
Phase 5
Phase 4
Phase 3
Phase 2
Phase 1
Phase 4 extension
Phase 7
Annexes

500 M

▼	Entrance/gate		📖	School			Block
🏠	Camp administration/ management		👫	Child-friendly space			Camp infrastructure
NGO	UN/NGO office		🏠	Distribution center			Phase
✚	Health facility		🔧	Service			
🗂	Market		☾	Mosque			
🏠	Community area (social)		🗼	Water tower			
			⠿	Sports field			

SOURCE: REACH, 2020d.

27

at al-Hol, AANES and SDF officials have explored the option of moving some of the women and children from the al-Hol foreigners' annex to Roj. Indeed, a camp extension to accommodate an additional 395 households opened in August 2020, and the SDF has transferred at least 92 foreign families from al-Hol to Roj.[11] By June 2021, Roj's population had increased to more than 2,500, with 84 percent being foreigners, or approximately 2,100 people.[12]

Roj provides a variety of services to inhabitants, although the camp is stressed because of limited resources and security concerns (see Figure 3.3). The camp has only one clinic, whose medical staff cannot treat complex medical needs, and 46 percent of camp residents reported encountering financial and accessibility barriers to obtaining medical care.[13] As of late 2020, NGOs operated one makeshift school with an attached child-friendly area in Roj, according to AANES officials, and there was also a vocational training center in the camp.[14]

Additional Camps

In addition to al-Hol and Roj, the Ain Issa camp—which was located at a retrofitted cotton factory about 60 kilometers north of ar-Raqqah—also previously accommodated foreign displaced persons. In late 2019, the Ain Issa camp comprised approximately 13,000 residents, including 1,000 foreigners. The camp was relatively well-established, organized into a "sprawling grid complete with shops, cafeterias, falafel stands, schools, clinics, mosques, a full-time administration, and offices of more than two dozen local and international NGOs."[15] However, following the October 2019 Turkish incursion into northeastern Syria and reports of Turkish forces shelling the camp, many of the residents—including some 950 non-Syrians living in a foreigners' annex—fled the camp. The SDF moved some of the foreigners to al-Hol, but the location of the majority of the Ain Issa camp's

---

[11] Rights and Security International, 2021, p. 13.

[12] U.S. Department of Defense, Office of Inspector General, 2021b, p. 80.

[13] Rights and Security International, 2021, p. 28; REACH, 2020e.

[14] Interview with a Kurdish official, phone, December 21, 2020; REACH, 2020e.

[15] Luke Mogelson, "America's Abandonment of Syria," *New Yorker*, April 20, 2020.

FIGURE 3.3
Map of Roj Camp

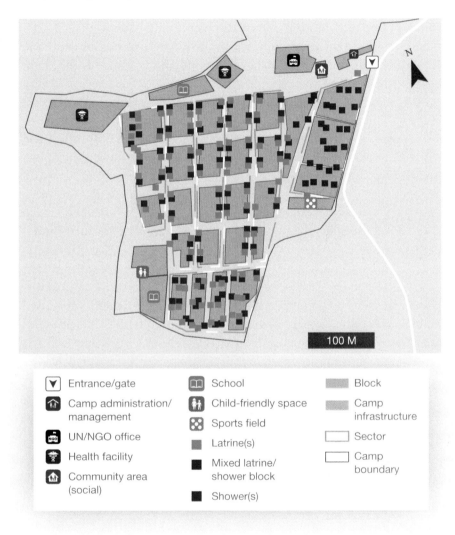

▼ Entrance/gate	📖 School	Block		
🏠 Camp administration/ management	👫 Child-friendly space	Camp infrastructure		
NGO UN/NGO office	Sports field	Sector		
Health facility	Latrine(s)	Camp boundary		
Community area (social)	Mixed latrine/ shower block			
	Shower(s)			

SOURCE: REACH, 2020e.

residents remains unclear, and the camp is no longer in operation.[16] With a history of breakouts from other camps, human smuggling from al-Hol, and ISIS's experience with conducting prison breaks, the risk of presumed ISIS-affiliated camp residents leaving remains high.

Several other IDP camps operate in northeastern Syria. For instance, the Mahmoudli camp in ar-Raqqah Province hosts nearly 8,200 IDPs, the Abu Khashab camp in Deir ez-Zor Province hosts nearly 9,400 IDPs, and the Areesheh camp in Hasakeh Province hosts nearly 13,000 IDPs.[17] Additionally, many thousands more reside in informal IDP settlements or in the region's urban areas.[18] However, these additional IDP camps and informal settlements do not contain significant numbers of displaced foreign individuals, if any.

The Full Extent of the ISIS Presence in the Camps Is Unclear

It is important to emphasize the great level of variability in ideological disposition across camp populations, especially among the foreign women and children. The 11,000 foreigners held at al-Hol arrived from Baghouz, where they remained with ISIS during the group's last stand. U.S. security officials warned of the "uncontested spread" of ISIS ideology and characterized two-thirds of camp residents as "ISIS supporters."[19]

The reality, however, is much more complex. Al-Hol and Roj undeniably include ardent ISIS supporters who continue to espouse ISIS ideol-

---

[16] "Ain Issa . . . From a Cotton Factory to a Camp of Thousands of IDPs" ["عين عيسى
. . . من مستودع أقطان إلى مخيم آلاف النازحين"], *Asharq Al-Awsat*, October 13, 2019; Louisa Loveluck, Souad Mekhennet, Loveday Morris, and Alice Martins, "Castaways from the Islamic State," *Washington Post*, December 24, 2019; International Crisis Group, 2019, p. 3.

[17] REACH, "Camp Profile: Mahmoudli," fact sheet, February 2020a; REACH, "Camp Profile: Abu Khashab," fact sheet, July 2020b; REACH, "Camp Profile: Areesheh," fact sheet, September 2020c.

[18] United Nations Office for the Coordination of Humanitarian Affairs, 2019b.

[19] U.S. Department of Defense, Office of Inspector General, 2019a, p. 24.

ogy and attempt to enforce the group's draconian rule on other camp residents (discussed in Chapters Two and Four). However, many other displaced persons—including the large majority of Syrian and Iraqi camp residents—do not openly support ISIS. As one International Crisis Group report affirms, even among the foreign population in al-Hol, "the militant women appear to be only a fraction within this population. Others have a more nuanced backstory," having been coerced into joining the group or traveled to Syria with their families or husbands.[20] Additionally, according to extremism expert Vera Mironova, many foreign women "feel they were used by ISIS's leadership to realize its political goals and do not believe in the group anymore."[21] Furthermore, open support for ISIS is noticeably lower at the Roj camp than at al-Hol. The group's advocates there are reportedly a "distinct minority" among the camp's foreign population, and most women are more relaxed and less adherent to dogmatic ISIS principles, such as austere black abayas for women.[22]

Nevertheless, despite being a minority, ISIS supporters remain active in both camps and particularly in al-Hol, and because of their forceful—and at times violent—methods, they might have an outsized influence and effect on life in the foreigners' annex. Their continued presence, especially without a thorough assessment of the extent of radicalization, threatens the delivery of services in the camps, camp security, justice, and repatriation efforts.

For a comparison with IDP camps in Iraq, see the box "A Comparison with Internally Displaced Persons Camps in Iraq." A brief review of the displacement crisis in Iraq provides a warning for northeastern Syria if the displacement crisis and the resulting humanitarian and security factors are not genuinely addressed.

---

[20] International Crisis Group, 2019, p. 5.

[21] International Crisis Group, 2019, p. 5; Vera Mironova, "Life Inside Syria's al-Hol Camp," Middle East Institute, July 9, 2020.

[22] International Crisis Group, 2019, p. 6.

A Comparison with Internally Displaced Persons Camps in Iraq

As in northeastern Syria, Iraq is also grappling with a displacement crisis that presents significant legal, social, and security challenges to the country's formal and informal governance system. Iraq experienced a huge surge of displacement during the 2014–2019 counter-ISIS campaign, forcing more than 6 million Iraqis from their homes. Approximately 4.85 million have returned, but of the remaining displaced population, at least 330,000 Iraqis are in IDP camps concentrated in the northern governorates of Ninewa, Dohuk, and Erbil.[a] The Federal Government of Iraq in Baghdad gradually worked to return camp residents to their communities of origin to close or consolidate camps. It expedited efforts in 2020, and by December of that year it had closed all but three camps; those camps were housing 26,000 IDPs. Around 180,000 IDPs remain in camps in the Kurdish Region of Iraq, and Kurdish authorities have not pursued expedited closure programs.[b]

Analysts and aid workers we interviewed in late 2020 warned that premature camp closures could force Iraqi IDPs into an even more uncertain, and potentially unsafe, status; their caution proved prescient because some IDPs returned to destroyed villages without basic infrastructure or security.[c] Multiple and interrelated factors contribute to IDPs' inability to return home, both those who were persecuted by ISIS and fled the group's expansion and those with perceived ISIS affiliations. First, many IDPs' homes were destroyed in the fighting, giving them nowhere to return to. Next, many IDPs lack government-issued documents and cannot obtain the security clearances necessary to pass through Iraq's myriad security hurdles to return.[d] Finally, significant numbers of IDPs fear returning to hostile, untrusting communities that assume returnees to be ISIS affiliates.

Other IDPs who have no ISIS ties and come from minority groups—such as the Yazidis or Shabaks—fear persecution from neighboring communities and might be reluctant to return to their communities of origin. Conversely, in areas such as Sinjar, armed groups affiliated with minority communities have prevented other IDPs from returning—especially those with perceived connections to ISIS. Therefore, Iraqi IDPs are at risk of secondary displacement—unable to remain in camps and unable to return to their homes. Because the majority of Iraqis residing in camps are women and children and secondary displacement puts them at risk of further societal marginalization, women-headed households without familial and social support networks are often stigmatized in Iraq.

Without sufficient government support or plans for returning IDPs to their homes and ensuring their safety, hundreds of thousands of Iraqis are at risk of becoming a permanently marginalized population without traditional social support networks, livelihoods, or education opportunities. Baghdad has not established a good national-level solution for justice, leaving situations for families with perceived ISIS affiliations to be variable. As part of the security clearance and resettlement process, approval from the *mukhtar*—a local community leader—is typically required; the mukhtar vouches for the good conduct of returning IDPs and guarantees their safety from reprisals. However, some mukhtars have been unable to guarantee returnees' safety because of communal hostility driven by perceived returnee ties to ISIS. Such perceptions and suspicions present a major impediment to safe return because many IDPs in camps have at least tertiary familial connections to ISIS members—although familial ties should not connote stigmatization of being an "ISIS family."[a] Iraq's security clearance process is also opaque and fraught with legal, social, and financial obstacles, further complicating IDPs' ability to leave camps with the necessary documentation and confidence that Iraqi security actors will allow them to return to their places of origin.

Of note, some of the IDPs in camps almost certainly still support ISIS. However, the group's clout has reportedly waned, and none of the experts interviewed for this study observed heightened support for ISIS in IDP camps. Nevertheless, their liminal status from real or perceived ties to ISIS makes them an increasingly vulnerable population, and unless they are properly reintegrated into Iraqi society, myriad armed groups—such the Popular Mobilization Units, the Kurdistan Workers' Party, and ISIS—and criminal actors could prey upon them and increase the risk of militarization.

---

[a] International Organization for Migration, "Displacement Tracking Matrix: Iraq Mission," webpage, February 28, 2021; International Crisis Group, *Exiles in Their Own Country: Dealing with Displacement in Post-ISIS Iraq*, Crisis Group Middle East Briefing No. 79, Brussels, October 19, 2020, p. 2.

[b] Samya Kullab, "Camp Closures Force Iraqi Families Back to Shattered Homes," Associated Press, December 16, 2020.

[c] Interview with an NGO worker, Washington, D.C., November 6, 2020; interview with an NGO worker, phone, November 16, 2020; interview with an academic, phone, November 20, 2020. Firas Al Khateeb, "Returning Iraqis Face Dire Conditions Following Camp Closures," UNHCR, May 27, 2021.

[d] Louisa Loveluck and Mustafa Salim, "Iraq Wants Thousands Displaced by the ISIS War to Go Home. They May Be Killed if They Do," *Washington Post*, December 22, 2020; for a detailed analysis on security clearance processes required of Iraqi IDPs, see International Crisis Group, 2020, and Alexandra Saieh and Naomi Petersohn, *Paperless People of Post-Conflict Iraq: Denied Rights, Barred from Basic Services and Excluded from Reconstruction Efforts*, Oslo: Norwegian Refugee Council, September 16, 2019.

[e] Interview with an NGO worker, Washington, D.C., November 6, 2020.

Summary

Both the living and security situations remain inadequate and unsafe for the tens of thousands of residents, predominately women and children, in al-Hol and Roj. As of late June 2021, al-Hol's population was just under 60,000 inhabitants, with Syrians at 34 percent (approximately 20,400), Iraqis at 51 percent (approximately 30,600), and foreigners at 15 percent (approximately 9,000). Roj contains 2,500 residents, with 84 percent (approximately 2,100) being foreigners and the remainder being Iraqis and Syrians.[23] In both camps, approximately two-thirds of the residents are children (approximately 40,200 at al-Hol and approximately 1,675 at Roj).[24] Obviously, not all residents of al-Hol and Roj are ISIS-affiliated, even those who are foreigners. However, the full extent of radicalization and ISIS affiliation remains unknown because of the security and resource constraints that prevent an assessment. Anecdotal evidence indicates that some former ISIS wives, and likely their children, are disillusioned and no longer support the group or its ideology. However, some women residing in the al-Hol foreigners' annex, in particular, actively support ISIS goals and attempt to establish governance

---

[23] U.S. Department of Defense, Office of Inspector General, 2021b, p. 80.

[24] U.S. Department of Defense, Office of Inspector General, 2021b, p. 18.

and education systems in the style of the group, along with spreading ISIS propaganda and punishing those who do not follow the group's standards. ISIS affiliation within the camps might be less than feared, but the presence of a core of adherents represents a security risk to other camp residents, NGO officials working within the camps, and AANES and SDF officials providing security. Moreover, those children still being raised in accordance with ISIS's dictates can still become fighters for the group once they reach adulthood. **Efforts to safely determine the full extent of ISIS support and membership must be undertaken to provide targeted solutions and to ensure that the entire camp or annex population is not punished for the beliefs and actions of a potential few.**

Iraqi refugees remaining in al-Hol and Roj continue to highlight the impact of refugees living in the camps. Baghdad faces policy issues about repatriating families with perceived ISIS affiliations and has not found good solutions. Some practices are similar to those implemented by the AANES and SDF, which are working with local communities to guarantee the safety of the families and communities. However, politicians and many communities do not want refugees to return from Syria, which is compounded by the lack of solutions for those who remain internally displaced by the counter-ISIS campaign and have limited options for returning home. **The United States, the Global Coalition to Defeat ISIS, the European Union, and the United Nations should provide the resources and expertise to AANES, SDF, and Iraqi officials to establish appropriate security vetting practices for the return of Syrians and Iraqis. Moreover, efforts to work with local communities to alleviate security concerns should be implemented.**

CHAPTER FOUR

Humanitarian Challenges and Risks

In this chapter, we review the humanitarian challenges and risks associated with the IDP camps in Kurdish-controlled displacement camps in Syria, and particularly al-Hol. Specifically, we consider conditions related to sanitation and health care, education, mental health, and access to employment in the camps. We chose these issues because they are the most critical for physical survival and maintaining emotional resilience, along with being basic ethical and moral responsibilities. Moreover, when deficits in these areas are combined with security factors, the risk for recruitment and radicalization increases, although research does not show that these factors individually increase the vulnerability. We then compare these circumstances with circumstances and risks in other similar camps elsewhere in the world.

Sanitation and Health Care Resources Remain Scarce and Insufficient

Even by the standards of displacement camps—which regularly cope with shortages in medical services and challenges in providing basic human needs—the northeastern Syrian camps' conditions are poor. Both al-Hol and Roj lack sufficient resources to keep inhabitants healthy, placing inhabitants, health workers, and security forces at risk. Overcrowded and unhygienic living conditions compromise physical health and increase discontent. ISIS can leverage the continued poor living conditions as propaganda and recruitment material.

The humanitarian situation in al-Hol is especially dire, with insufficient facilities and services to provide for the camp's nearly 67,000 residents. The need for humanitarian assistance, although still great, was arguably most acute following the major wave of displacement in March 2019, when thousands of small children arrived in the camp exhausted and malnourished. Indeed, the International Rescue Committee recorded 142 deaths of children under the age of five by March 15, 2019, and another 313 deaths by September 2019.[1] During this period, around 35 aid organizations worked in al-Hol, providing malnutrition screening for the thousands of IDPs, foreign children, and adults in addition to water, sanitation, and hygiene (WASH) assistance to the broader camp population.

Inadequate sanitation and waste management in the camp increases the risk of spreading diseases. For instance, an insufficient number of waste receptacles has resulted in garbage strewn throughout the camps and on walking paths. Sewage drainage is also inadequate and overflows, particularly in the summer months, and at times leaks into tents.[2] Camp residents also experience sanitation issues with communal latrines, which lack lighting and sufficient water for sanitation. Some residents have dug private pits to serve as latrines, which can compound the camp's sewage problems.[3]

Sanitation and waste management issues might already be contributing to the spread of disease and death within the Syrian camps. Typhoid and other diseases have spread in al-Hol.[4] Although these outbreaks have not yet resulted in a significant death toll, the situation could get worse without increased investment in improving access to proper sanitation and waste management. The northeastern Syrian camps' displaced population's exposure to and spread of disease have not as of yet been as dire as past displacement experiences, such as the 1994 cholera outbreaks among Rwandan refugees in the Democratic Republic of the Congo, which killed an estimated

---

[1] International Rescue Committee, "Data Analyzed by the IRC Reveals Staggering Health and Humanitarian Needs of Children in Al Hol Camp, Northeast Syria—Urging Repatriation of Foreign Children," press release, al-Hol, Syria, September 16, 2019.

[2] Louisa Loveluck, "In Syrian Camp for Women and Children Who Left ISIS Caliphate, a Struggle Even to Register Names," *Washington Post,* June 28, 2020.

[3] Interview with a Syrian Democratic Council official, phone, December 21, 2020; REACH, 2020d.

[4] Syrians for Truth and Justice, 2018; World Health Organization, "Syria Crisis—WHO's Response in Al-Hol Camp, Al-Hasakeh Governorate, Issue 13, 2–15 August 2019," October 3, 2019.

50,000 refugees in three months.[5] This should not be taken as reason to not improve the current situation, but as a warning that endemic spread of disease within a displaced persons camp can occur rather quickly given the right conditions. In July 1994, Rwandan refugees settled in camps without an adequate supply of clean water, sanitation planning or systems, or medical treatment. They relied on Lake Kivu's untreated water for "drinking, bathing, and washing clothes," and within the month, a cholera outbreak spread through the camps.[6] The mortality rate declined significantly after October 1994, primarily because of NGOs' efforts to establish better sanitation and health care in the refugee camps.[7]

Humanitarian health concerns in the camps became even more acute amid the coronavirus disease 2019 (COVID-19) pandemic. Al-Hol is more than 150 percent over capacity, with a density approximately three times greater than Manhattan; therefore, social distancing is exceedingly difficult and only minimally practiced.[8] Moreover, al-Hol reportedly lacks sufficient sanitation and handwashing stations to help avert community spread of COVID-19 and other diseases.[9] Aid workers reported the first cases of COVID-19 in the camp in August 2020; however, through mid-2021, the camp had not yet experienced a significant COVID-19 outbreak. Nevertheless, the COVID-19 crisis has had second-order detrimental effects in the camp, with aid organizations temporarily shuttering their clinics because of COVID-19 concerns, further limiting camp residents' access to needed health care. Because the camp was already suffering from insufficient medical services and humanitarian aid, OIG warned at the end of 2020 that "due to COVID-19 mitigation measures, however, humanitarian access and

---

[5] Sarah Kanyon Lischer, *Dangerous Sanctuaries: Refugee Camps, Civil War, and the Dilemmas of Humanitarian Aid,* Ithaca, N.Y.: Cornell University Press, 2005, pp. 79, 91, 95.

[6] Gillian McKay and Melissa Parker, "Epidemics," in Tim Allen, Anna Macdonald, and Henry Radice, eds., *Humanitarianism: A Dictionary of Concepts,* New York: Routledge, 2018, pp. 82–83; Lischer, 2005, pp. 79, 91, 95.

[7] Lischer, 2005, pp. 79, 90, 91, 95.

[8] Rights and Security International, 2021, p. 12; REACH, 2020d.

[9] REACH, 2020d.

assistance at the camp continues to be restricted to life-saving humanitarian assistance such as food, water, sanitation, health care, and shelter."[10]

The humanitarian situation in the Roj camp is also concerning; however, because of the camp's significantly smaller size—relative to al-Hol—certain types of WASH aid and services provided are less restricted. For instance, the availability of latrines and showers meets minimum humanitarian standards, and garbage and solid waste are collected twice a day—whereas in al-Hol, insufficient garbage and waste collection present major health risks.[11] However, like al-Hol, Roj also lacks sufficient medical services.

Inadequate Educational Services Increase Risks of Radicalization

Because of logistical hurdles and limited capacity—even before the constraints added by the COVID-19 pandemic—NGOs in the camps cannot provide formal education, meaning that children are not learning in consistent, structured environments with standardized resources. Rather, the rudimentary education activities—often in "self-learning" environments geared toward fostering basic numeracy and literacy—aim to provide some intellectual stimulation and foundational knowledge on which the children can build once they leave the camps at some unknown future date and can access formal schooling.[12] Research has also shown that quality and quantity of educational opportunities can have an impact on future radicalization trends.

Educational services are rudimentary and provide limited instruction in math, science, Arabic, and English to children ages three to 17. Only 40 percent of children in al-Hol and 88 percent of children in Roj receive this basic

---

[10] Agathe Christien, Emma Jouenne, and Elena Scott-Kakures, "How COVID-19 Underscores the Urgent Need to Repatriate Women and Children from Northeast Syria Camps," Georgetown Institute for Women, Peace and Security, December 9, 2020; Médecins Sans Frontières, 2020; U.S. Department of Defense, Office of Inspector General, 2020c, p. 70.

[11] REACH, 2020e.

[12] United Nations Office for the Coordination of Humanitarian Affairs, "Syria: Humanitarian Response in Al Hol Camp," Situation Report No. 2, April 20, 2019a, p. 6.

education, meaning that approximately 27,000 children are not receiving any instruction at all.[13] Indeed, some parents in al-Hol who were dissatisfied with the quality and pace of education provided in the NGO-run schools started organizing their own educational services, although some children have complained that the instruction is not challenging enough.[14] In al-Hol, because of security concerns and the restricted nature of the foreigners' annex, Syrian and Iraqi children receive instruction separate from foreign children.[15] Furthermore, the myriad of nationalities and languages spoken by al-Hol's foreign population presents difficulties in providing educational services to the foreign children and inhibits aid workers' ability to provide all children the same level of education.[16] Countries that host Syrian refugees often grapple with similar issues. Efforts to educate Syrian refugees in Jordan, Lebanon, and Turkey face logistical challenges such as space shortages and overcrowding, limited teacher expertise, poor curricula, and language barriers, preventing strong educational offerings.[17]

Access to education in camps has historically been difficult, with some host countries (and even UNHCR at times) placing barriers to education. This could be done in an effort to encourage refugees to return to their

---

[13] Interview with an NGO worker, phone, January 14, 2021; REACH, 2020e; REACH, 2020d. Historically, refugee access to education is not unlike that experienced in northeastern Syria. In 2018, UNHCR reported that 63 percent of refugee children were enrolled in primary education, but only 24 percent were enrolled in secondary schools. Although refugees might face barriers emplaced by NGOs, UNHCR, or host countries, concerns about students receiving education might discourage families from returning home. See UNHCR, *Stepping Up: Refugee Education in Crisis*, Geneva, Switzerland, September 2019; Lyndsay Bird, *Surviving School: Education for Refugee Children from Rwanda 1994–1996*, Paris: International Institute for Educational Planning, 2003, p. 19.

[14] Interview with an NGO worker, phone, January 14, 2021.

[15] Interview with an NGO worker, phone, January 14, 2021.

[16] Interview with an NGO worker, phone, January 14, 2021.

[17] Shelly Culbertson and Louay Constant, *Education of Syrian Refugee Children: Managing the Crisis in Turkey, Lebanon, and Jordan*, Santa Monica, Calif.: RAND Corporation, RR-859-CMEPP, 2015; Shelly Culbertson, Tom Ling, Marie-Louise Henham, Jennie Corbett, Rita T. Karam, Paulina Pankowska, Catherine L. Saunders, Jacopo Bellasio, and Ben Baruch, *Evaluation of the Emergency Education Response for Syrian Refugee Children and Host Communities in Jordan*, Santa Monica, Calif: RAND Corporation, RR-1203-UNICF, 2016.

home countries, as with Rwandan refugees in the Democratic Republic of the Congo in the mid-1990s.[18] Or barriers to education might be in place because of security concerns, as with Sri Lankan Tamil refugees in India in the early 1990s.[19] However, in both instances, access to education was ultimately provided to refugees. In other instances, such as with Afghan refugees in Pakistan, lack of access could be exacerbated by poor educational systems in the host country.[20] Ultimately, uneven access and application to education harms children living in the camps and limits their future opportunities.

Education is one humanitarian factor that might have a more direct impact on the risk of radicalization. According to Save the Children, education can promote peace and economic prosperity or future violence and conflict through its role in promoting national identities and common knowledge standards.[21] ISIS, not unlike other nonstate armed groups, focused on educating children in the so-called caliphate as a way not only to ensure the continuation of the group's existence but also to buttress its governance capabilities.[22] The ISIS curriculum removed liberal arts subjects—history, geography, literature—while illustrating math problems with weapons and calculating the results of a suicide bombing.[23] Limited access to educational resources for children in the camps, both those with and without ISIS affiliations, will have reverberating effects on them, their families, and broader communities and economies as they grow up.

---

[18] Bird, 2003, pp. 77–78.

[19] Prakash M. Swamy, "Sri Lankan Tamil Students Denied Admission to Educational Institutions in Tamil Nadu," *India Today*, February 15, 1992.

[20] Amnesty International, "Afghanistan's Refugees: Forty Years of Dispossession," June 20, 2019.

[21] Save the Children, *Rewrite the Future: Education for Children in Conflict-Affected Countries*, London, 2006.

[22] Richard C. Baffa, Nathan Vest, Wing Yi Chan, and Abby Fanlo, *Defining and Understanding the Next Generation of Salafi-Jihadis*, Santa Monica, Calif.: RAND Corporation, PE-341-ODNI, 2019; United Nations Office on Drugs and Crime, *Handbook on Children Recruited and Exploited by Terrorist and Violent Extremist Groups: The Role of the Justice System*, Vienna, 2017.

[23] Shelly Culbertson, "The Urgent Need for an Education Plan in Mosul," *RAND Blog*, March 27, 2017.

Moreover, parents might be a primary vector for radicalizing children in al-Hol or Roj. U.S. officials, researchers, and aid workers have warned of the potential for pro-ISIS women in al-Hol to radicalize youth in the camp, stating that should the child—especially those in al-Hol and Roj's foreign annexes—remain arbitrarily detained with no outlets, the camps could become a "petri dish" and "prime condition for radicalization."[24] Jessica Trisko Darden argues that one of the major pathways by which youth radicalize is "personal connections, including family and friendship networks," and some camp residents have actively attempted to expose children to pro-ISIS ideology.[25] Some parents are conducting ISIS-style instruction in private, both to instill the group's ideology in their children and because of their aversion to NGOs' Western-style educational practices.[26] Additionally, some women have encouraged their children to throw rocks and act belligerently toward camp guards. Others have played pro-ISIS media around children, possibly with the intent to "preserve the next generation of militants."[27]

Mental Health Services Are Lacking, Compounding Preexisting Trauma

Compounding the problem of limited educational services, there is a lack of mental health support in the camps because of the same overarching issues related to security, limited logistical support, and COVID-19 restrictions. Human Rights Watch noted in March 2021 that "almost no [. . .] counsel-

---

[24] U.S. Department of Defense, Office of Inspector General, 2019a, p. 41; interview with NGO workers, phone, November 25, 2020.

[25] Jessica Trisko Darden, *Tackling Terrorists' Exploitation of Youth*, Washington, D.C.: American Enterprise Institute, May 2019. A study by Haer and Hecker, looking at Congolese refugees in Uganda, found that individuals are more likely to be approached for recruitment if someone in their personal network is associated with a militant group. See Haer and Hecker, 2019.

[26] Zelin, 2019, p. 4.

[27] International Crisis Group, 2019; Mironova, 2020.

ing for a severely traumatized population" was available in al-Hol.[28] The International Rescue Committee provides mental health services through all of its clinics and hospitals in northeastern Syria, but it is unknown how COVID-19 restrictions and the security situation in the camps have affected the International Rescue Committee's ability to currently provide health services.[29] Leaving the emotional and mental health of camp residents unaddressed is problematic, because, upon arrival to al-Hol and Roj, adults and children were already traumatized from living through the Syrian Civil War and/or ISIS's so-called caliphate. Living in the camps can continue to provide traumatizing experiences. Ignoring this trauma makes camp inhabitants more vulnerable to recruitment and radicalization.

All of the children in al-Hol and Roj have been affected by conflict, disrupting their access to formal education and hampering their cognitive development. Many of the youth have likely also witnessed instances of violence, which might have detrimental psychological effects on them, and some might have even been indoctrinated by ISIS as part of the Cubs and Pearls of the Caliphate.[30] Such psychological stressors have been linked to heightened aggression and emotional withdrawal among youth, possibly making them more susceptible to radicalization and militarization. In their 2003 study on trauma and the effects of violent experiences on child development, Paramjit T. Joshi and Deborah A. O'Donnell assert that "exposure to increased levels of violence leads to decreased sensitivity to violence and a greater willingness to tolerate increasing levels of aggression and violence in society,"[31] often resulting in heightened aggression, depression, and stunted cognitive development in children.[32] Therefore, educational activities and mental health services designed to mitigate antisocial behavior, encourage

---

[28] Human Rights Watch, "Thousands of Foreigners Unlawfully Held in NE Syria," March 23, 2021.

[29] International Rescue Committee, "NE Syria: 60% Increase in COVID-19 Cases in Past Week, IRC Calls for Increased Health Capacity," press release, New York, August 17, 2020.

[30] See Baffa et al., 2019.

[31] Paramjit T. Joshi and Deborah A. O'Donnell, "Consequences of Child Exposure to War and Terrorism," *Clinical Child and Family Psychology Review*, Vol. 6, No. 4, December 2003, p. 280.

[32] Joshi and O'Donnell, 2003, p. 275.

critical thinking, and encourage empathy could at least reduce the suscepti-
bility of al-Hol and Roj's youth to radicalization.[33]

Any modicum of education and intellectual stimulation might prove
vital for children in the camps. In particular, educational activities could
minimize cognitive atrophy and developmental breaks and provide some
educational foundation upon which to build once they leave the displacement camps. Moreover, education and intellectual stimulation might also
reduce aggressive and violent behavior and the risk of radicalization. Indeed,
NGOs have reported children exhibiting indicators of posttraumatic stress
because of their experiences in the war. For instance, some children have
become emotionally withdrawn, irresponsive, and apathetic, and some
mothers have reported grappling with extremely erratic behavior from their
children.[34] NGOs such as Save the Children are implementing "child protection activities," which entail child-friendly spaces and protection monitoring. These are not deradicalization activities, nor do they provide educational instruction. However, they are intended to provide safe spaces in
which children can decompress.[35]

Living in poverty and/or displaced persons camps does not mean that
a person will inevitably radicalize, but when combined with other factors, this environment can influence a person's vulnerability. Extremist
groups have taken advantage of poor living conditions and a perceived lack
of opportunity when recruiting new members; these elements do exist for
al-Hol and Roj's inhabitants. When combined with the security challenges
and policy decisions that often isolate and punish refugees and IDPs, the
risk of extremist views becoming more appealing could increase.

---

[33] Lawrence Kuznar, Ali Jafri, and Eric Kuznar, *Dealing with Radicalization in IDP
Camps*, Boston, Mass.: NSI, February 2020, p. 6.

[34] Rights and Security International conveyed the struggles that one mother faced
with her three-year-old son who regularly inflicted self-harm and still needed to wear
a diaper. See Rights and Security International, 2021, pp. 4, 23; Monica Awad and Delil
Soulieman, "Child-Friendly Spaces Offer Respite for Raqqa's Displaced Children,"
UNICEF, August 23, 2017; REACH, 2020e, p. 3.

[35] Save the Children, "Repatriation of Foreign Children in Syria Slowed by COVID-19,
as New Footage Emerges of Life in Camps," February 1, 2021; interview with an NGO
worker, phone, January 14, 2021.

Access to Employment Is Inadequate and Limited by Poor Freedom of Movement

Access to employment for residents of al-Hol and Roj is variable. Although internal camp economies exist, including the opportunity to work for NGOs, the camps' locations—away from population centers—limit movement and options for employment. A lack of job opportunities can increase feelings of isolation and increases reliance on a smuggling black market (discussed further in Chapter Five), which can be leveraged by ISIS to induce continued support for the group.

Few employment opportunities are available in al-Hol, and many families struggle to make ends meet. Some camp residents are able to work as low-skill services laborers, and others have found employment in the camp's markets. However, steady employment is scarce, and many residents financially cope by selling their few remaining assets or borrowing money.[36] Additionally, as mentioned earlier, in some instances pro-ISIS women "marry" foreign group supporters who, in turn, provide the women and their children money to subsist on or to escape the camp. Opportunities for employment appear to be better in Roj than in al-Hol, and 63 percent of residents reporting a source of household income indicated that they were able to find employment within the camp. Low-skilled labor still accounts for the major source of jobs inside Roj, at 68 percent of reported employment categories; however, nearly a quarter of Roj residents have some form of private business, such as shopkeeping.[37]

At al-Hol and, to a lesser extent, Roj, lack of economic opportunities and poor integration into the local economy can increase residents' feelings of isolation, injustice, and inadequacy in being able to provide for their families. This is a familiar scenario for refugees—in both camps and informal settlements—and is often the result of policy decisions designed to prevent refugees from staying long-term and to protect local employment opportunities. However, the primary result is the continued isolation of displaced people, exacerbating their vulnerability. In most countries, refugees struggle to find a job, or they often take on informal or irregular work, such as

---

[36] REACH, 2020d, p. 2.

[37] REACH 2020e, p. 5.

when a host nation restricts the legal right to work among those living in the camps. For example, Palestinian refugees in Lebanon are limited to specific jobs so that they do not compete with Lebanese citizens.[38] In Kenya, the government does not allow refugees to join the workforce at all.[39] These measures can drive displaced people to become active participants in informal economies to maintain an income while further isolating them from the societies in which they are living.[40]

Summary

We found that although the international aid community has a humanitarian requirement to ensure that residents have proper and consistent access to nutrition, sanitation and hygiene, and medical and educational services, conditions are not meeting adequate humanitarian standards. Difficulties in not providing these services reliably could serve to increase the influence of violent extremist groups such as ISIS that operate both within the camp and its surrounding area and increase resentment against governing authorities. In addition, the lack of services from aid groups and governing authorities could increase the legitimacy and influence of militant groups who are able to, in some cases, better provide such services. Such was the case in Afghanistan, where local populations readily took whatever assistance was available, regardless of whether it came from the local govern-

---

[38] Jad Chaaban, Nisreen Salti, Hala Ghattas, Alexandra Irani, Tala Ismail, and Lara Batlouni, *Survey on the Socioeconomic Status of Palestine Refugees in Lebanon 2015,* American University of Beirut and the United Nations Relief and Works Agency for Palestine Refugees in the Near East, 2016.

[39] Norwegian Refugee Council, *Supporting Kakuma's Refugees: The Importance of Freedom of Movement,* Oslo, August 2018; David McKenzie and Brent Swails, "Sanctuary Without End: The Refugees the World Forgot," *CNN,* October 2015.

[40] Dany Bahar and Meagan Dooley, "No Refugees and Migrants Left Behind," in Homi Kharas, John W. McArthur, and Izumi Ohno, eds., *Leave No One Behind: Time for Specifics on the Sustainable Development Goals,* Washington, D.C.: Brookings Institution Press, 2019.

ment or Taliban militants.[41] **To avert a broader humanitarian catastrophe in al-Hol and Roj, the Counter-ISIS Coalition, the United Nations, the European Union, and other major international donors should invest significantly in establishing quality sanitation and health care infrastructure and expertise for the camps operating within the territory for which the AANES and SDF maintain governance and security.**

Education and mental health services are also critical for improving refugee and IDP resilience against militant recruitment. Although parental—and peer—radicalization of children in al-Hol and Roj is a major security concern, it is important to note that influence and indoctrination are not unidirectional. As noted earlier, the majority of residents in both camps do not outwardly espouse ISIS ideology; therefore, more exposure to less-militant women and children could potentially have a moderating effect on children of pro-ISIS women. Limited examples demonstrate that foreign women in Roj, once separated from the most ideological pro-ISIS women, have reportedly begun to reject the principles of ISIS, highlighting the potential for moderation.[42] **Resources and expertise from the Counter-ISIS Coalition member countries, the United Nations, and the European Union are required to support the AANES and SDF in identifying and separating the less-militant women and children from those most radicalized by ISIS ideology.** To address the lack of mental health resources, we also recommend that **these same donors increase resources and expertise to the NGOs providing mental health services, along with developing a variety of services that are appropriate for the type of trauma experienced and tailored to the age of the camp resident.**

Access to employment opportunities remains critical not only for improving the current quality of life of camp residents but also for supporting efforts to facilitate their eventual departure and return to safe environments. Employment that meets and exceeds basic survival needs will also have the added benefit of making inhabitants less vulnerable to ISIS recruitment efforts as well. **The AANES and SDF must work with**

---

[41] Robert D. Lamb and Brooke Shawn, *Political Governance and Strategy in Afghanistan*, Washington, D.C.: Center for Strategic and International Studies, April 2012.

[42] Natalia Sancha, "The Transformation of ISIS Women in Syria's Al Roj Camp," *El País*, March 26, 2021.

the Counter-ISIS Coalition and NGO partners to integrate vetted camp inhabitants with local economies to provide employment opportunities. The safety of camp residents and local towns must be maintained, but increased freedom of movement will support economic development.

CHAPTER FIVE

Security Challenges and Risks

In this chapter, we review the physical security challenges facing the IDP and refugee camps in northeastern Syria and the risks they pose to camp inhabitants. Similar to the provision of humanitarian goods and services, providing safe and secure environments for IDPs and refugees is a core moral responsibility for the international community and aid organizations. It is also a key consideration for global antiviolent extremism efforts. Yet, as a 2021 Rights and Security International report articulates, the "al-Hol and Roj camps are fundamentally unsafe environments in which physical violence is common and psychological trauma is endemic."[1] Coupled with critical shortages of medical services, nutritional aid, humanitarian relief, and educational activities, the camps in northeastern Syria present significant security concerns that could deteriorate into full-blown crises the longer they remain unaddressed. Moreover, limited policing and security resources can contribute to radicalization rates, especially if the presence of a pre-radicalized group exists in camps, or if armed groups are able to take control of the camp.[2]

In this chapter, we discuss the impact of the limited security presence and oversight in the camps—including limited freedom of movement—and the connections ISIS maintains in al-Hol and Roj and the surrounding areas through activities including the smuggling of people and materiel. We will continue to provide examples of international cases as well.

---

[1] Rights and Security International, 2021, p. 19.

[2] Sude, Stebbins, and Weilant, 2015, pp. 10–11.

The Limited Security Service Presence Contributes to Increased Violence

Insecurity within al-Hol and Roj remains a critical concern and an issue that ISIS-affiliated members contribute to. The AANES and SDF have limited financial and physical resources to address the riots, petty crime, and violence between residents and against guards. In addition to the presence of ISIS within and around the camps, regional and international politics also negatively affect the provision of adequate funding and resources to support AANES and SDF efforts. Faced with constant insecurity, which is exploited by ISIS, people become more vulnerable to recruitment and radicalization to avoid living in a poor humanitarian situation, as laid out in the previous chapter.

The AANES oversees and manages al-Hol and Roj and partners with the camps' NGO administrator, Blumont. UNHCR and other international NGOs provide services and maintain a presence in the camps, although the AANES—through the SDF—provides security. This arrangement is not unlike that of other camps, such as in Bangladesh, Kenya, and Sri Lanka, although in northeastern Syria security is provided by the AANES, a non-state actor, while in the previous cases security appears to be provided by state or state-authorized authorities.[3] The AANES is not an internationally recognized governing entity and lacks the resources and infrastructure generally available to governments.

The AANES has struggled to provide appropriate levels of security in al-Hol and Roj, even with support from the United States and the Global Coalition to Defeat ISIS. Security services at al-Hol have generally comprised between 350 and 450 personnel—a mixture of Asayesh (Kurdish police) and YPG fighters—and have only been able to provide "min-

---

[3] On Bangladesh, see UNHCR, "Rohingya Refugee Response—Bangladesh—Operational Dashboard: 2020 Indicators Monitoring," infographic, July 31, 2020. On Kenya, see Moulid Hujale, "The Refugee Camp That Became a City," *New Humanitarian*, January 20, 2016. On Sri Lanka, see Tom Widger, "Philanthronationalism: Junctures at the Business–Charity Nexus in Post-War Sri Lanka," *Development and Change*, Vol. 47, No. 1, January 2016.

imal security around the camp's perimeters."[4] The Kurdish force posture at al-Hol has not increased since late 2019, despite U.S. and Counter-ISIS Coalition security assistance activities to train more SDF internal security forces. Additionally, regional security concerns—such as Turkey's October 2019 incursion—forced the SDF to redeploy some of al-Hol's guard units to active fronts, further limiting already tenuous camp security.[5] In late 2022, Turkey again threatened to invade northeastern Syria; the SDF warned that in the event of a Turkish incursion, they would not be able to continue to guard the camps.[6]

Intended to alleviate pressure on security forces and aid organizations working in al-Hol, the expedited release of Syrian IDPs from late 2020 onward began when ISIS was stepping up its activity inside al-Hol. Pro-ISIS residents in al-Hol reportedly killed 20 people in January 2021 alone, compared with 26 total murders in the second half of 2020, which targeted camp security personnel and residents working with camp administrators and services.[7] Additionally, ISIS has maintained a steady rate of attacks outside the camp in SDF-controlled areas of Deir ez-Zor, Hasakeh, and ar-Raqqah provinces, including assassinations, attacks on checkpoints, and planting road bombs.[8] In January 2022, ISIS launched an attack against and overran Ghuwayran Detention Facility in Hasakeh. A multi-day siege ensued before

---

[4] U.S. Department of Defense, Office of Inspector General, *Operation Inherent Resolve: Lead Inspector General Report to the United States Congress*, Alexandria, Va., January 1, 2020–March 31, 2020a, p. 53; U.S. Department of Defense, Office of Inspector General, 2019a, p. 24.

[5] Elizabeth Tsurkov and Dareen Khalifa, "An Unnerving Fate for the Families of Syria's Northeast," Carnegie Endowment for International Peace, January 31, 2020.

[6] Poonam Taneja and Jewan Abdi, "Islamic State: Kurdish Forces Threaten to Stop Guarding Camps," BBC News, November 25, 2022.

[7] "Killings on the Rise in Syria's al-Hol Camp," *Al-Monitor*, February 18, 2021; Rights and Security International, 2021, p. 19; U.S. Department of Defense, Office of Inspector General, 2020c, p. 68.

[8] Mohammed Hardan, "How Islamic State Returned to Haunt Civilians in Northeast Syria," *Al-Monitor*, February 22, 2021.

the SDF, with support from U.S. and coalition military forces, could regain control of the prison.[9]

Past instances of policing operations of the annex—purportedly to conduct biometric registration—have confined residents to their tents and limited them to only bread and water for days. Aid workers have warned of "collective punishment" of all annex residents for the actions of a few.[10] However, security sweeps have contributed to improved security conditions. In particular, a five-day sweep of al-Hol in March 2021 that involved more than 5,000 SDF personnel led to the arrest of 125 people tied to ISIS or violent activity in the camp and allowed for further biometric enrollment of camp residents. Moreover, in the month following the SDF's security sweep, camp authorities reported only one murder, compared with at least 47 in the first three months of 2021.[11] The SDF continued counter-ISIS security operations in al-Hol throughout 2022. In September 2022, the SDF and camp security forces disrupted an ISIS facilitation network based in the camp, arresting "dozens." Additionally, security forces rescued women chained and tortured in tunnels around al-Hol.[12]

Small-scale riots and violence against camp security services are relatively regular occurrences in al-Hol. For instance, a riot broke out in the foreigners' annex in September 2019 when Asayesh disrupted pro-ISIS women from establishing a Shari'a court and imposing ISIS-like rule in the annex. The Asayesh intervention led to one woman being killed, several more injured, and around 50 arrests.[13] Additionally, foreign women and children have assaulted guards and even aid workers in the camp. On at least two occasions, women have attacked guards with knives—stabbing a woman Asayesh guard to death in one incident. According to the International Crisis Group, the persistent violence, periodically directed toward aid work-

---

[9] Louisa Loveluck and Sarah Cahlan, "Prison Break: ISIS Fighters Launched a Brazen Attack to Free Their Comrades," *Washington Post*, February 3, 2022.

[10] Loveluck, 2020.

[11] U.S. Department of Defense, Office of Inspector General, 2021a, p. 18.

[12] Karoun Demirjian, "Raids on ISIS Camp in Syria Yield Hundreds of Arrests," *Washington Post*, September 7, 2022.

[13] Wladimir van Wilgenburg, "One Woman Killed After ISIS-Motivated Riot in Syria's al-Hol Camp," Kurdistan24, September 30, 2019.

ers, has "prevented aid groups from providing sufficient services," leaving annex residents without "adequate food, clean water, often cut off entirely from medical services."[14] Furthermore, there are also accounts of guards sexually assaulting women in the annex and taking advantage of their economic deprivation to exchange money for sex.[15]

Even the most secure camps can destabilize when outlying security conditions worsen. The Ain Issa camp was reportedly the best administered and most secure camp under the control of the AANES, with high-quality services and facilities, compared with al-Hol. However, during the October 2019 Turkish incursion, Ain Issa was caught in the crossfire between Turkish forces and their Syrian proxies fighting the SDF. Amid shelling and disruptions to camp security, nearly all 950 foreign women and children departed Ain Issa.[16] Additionally, as mentioned earlier, the Turkish incursion prompted the YPG component of the SDF to redeploy more than a third of its fighters guarding al-Hol to counter the Turkish offensive. With just a skeleton crew to guard al-Hol, approximately 200 women and children with ties to ISIS escaped.[17] The mass exodus from Ain Issa and high rate of escapes from al-Hol during the October 2019 crisis reflect the fragile nature of the camps' security and stability, which could again be jeopardized by future security crises in the area.

Previously in other countries, the deterioration or absence of security in camps has led to full-blown insurgencies erupting. In 2007, the Leba-

---

[14] Loveluck, 2020; International Crisis Group, 2019.

[15] Mironova, 2020; Rights and Security International, 2021, p. 20. Sexual violence is by no means uncommon in displacement camps. Furthermore, it is common for sexual violence to go unreported because of threats of reprisals against those raped, stigma associated with victims of sexual violence, belief that little will be done to punish the perpetrators, and other factors. See Laetitia Bader and Ben Rawlence, *Hostages of the Gatekeepers: Abuses Against Internally Displaced in Mogadishu, Somalia*, Human Rights Watch, March 2013; "Are Militants Tightening Grip on Rohingya Refugee Camps?" Deutsche Welle, September 24, 2019.

[16] "Ain Issa . . . From a Cotton Factory to a Camp of Thousands of IDPs" ["عين عيسى . . من مستودع أقطان إلى مخيم الآلاف النازحين"], 2019; Loveluck et al., 2019; International Crisis Group, 2019, p. 3.

[17] The SDF was able to capture and return more than 100 of the escapees to al-Hol. See Tsurkov and Khalifa, 2020.

nese Armed Forces waged a four-month-long operation to root out Fatah al-Islam, a Salafi-Jihadi militant group, from the Nahr al-Bared Palestinian refugee camp. Over the course of the siege, Palestinian factions, the Lebanese Armed Forces, and Fatah al-Islam failed to properly ensure the protection of the civilian population residing in the camp. An estimated 400 civilians were killed, and more than 1,000 were injured. Additionally, the fighting devastated the camp's infrastructure, which still has not been fully rebuilt.[18] This experience provides a cautionary tale for the camps in northeastern Syria if security is not maintained.

A Radicalized Population Conducts Violence Against Innocent Civilians

A unique element for the displaced populations in al-Hol and Roj was the arrival of the already radicalized population that emerged from Baghouz following ISIS's surrender of its final major safe haven in Syria. Historically, armed groups or their supporters generally have not arrived en masse with the displaced persons seeking refuge in the camps.[19] Over 60,000 women

---

[18] Samer Abboud, "The Siege of Nahr al-Bared and the Palestinian Refugees in Lebanon," *Arab Studies Quarterly*, Vol. 31, No. 1–2, Winter–Spring 2009; United Nations Relief and Works Agency for Palestine Refugees in the Near East, *Reconstruction of Nahr El-Bared Camp and UNRWA Compound*, Beirut, June 2012.

[19] If a conflict is ongoing, over time, armed groups and current or former members often create some sort of presence inside of the camps, at times with intent to recruit camp inhabitants. These armed groups might also use the camps as safe havens and a place of residence, usually placing nonaffiliated civilian inhabitants at risk. Armed groups have been present in refugee and IDP camps in Bangladesh, the Democratic Republic of the Congo, Lebanon, Somalia, Sri Lanka, and Tanzania. For more details, see "Are Militants Tightening Grip on Rohingya Refugee Camps?" 2019; Amnesty International, "Bangladesh: Rohingya Refugees' Safety Must Be Ensured Amid Violent Clashes in Cox's Bazaar," press release, October 9, 2020; Lischer, 2005; International Crisis Group, *Nurturing Instability: Lebanon's Palestinian Refugee Camps*, Middle East Report No. 84, Brussels, February 19, 2009; UNHCR, *The Situation of Palestinian Refugees in Lebanon*, Geneva, Switzerland, February 2016a; Bader and Rawlence, 2013; Abdalle Ahmed Mumin, "Somalia's Displacement Camp 'Gatekeepers'—'Parasites' or Aid Partners?" *New Humanitarian*, July 18, 2019; Amnesty International, "Sri Lanka: Armed Groups Infiltrating Refugee Camps," press release, London, March 14, 2007.

and children flooded al-Hol, but because of the security situation in the camps, an accurate assessment of current levels of ISIS affiliation is unavailable. Some of these women and children have renounced ISIS ideology. However, others have attempted to establish ISIS-like rule inside the camp and within the foreigners' annex, in particular, leading to myriad violent incidents including beatings and murders.[20] Additionally, some foreign women promote ISIS ideology on social media, in exchange for payment, and focus their efforts on children and teenagers.[21]

SDF authorities did initially attempt to separate those deemed a potential higher security risk by placing them in detention camps. As people relocated because of fighting throughout the 2015 to 2019 effort to territorially defeat ISIS in northeastern Syria, the SDF imprisoned suspected ISIS fighters and directed women and children, including teenagers, toward the camps.[22] This separation has precedence, as governments have separated armed group members from the general population of refugee and IDP camps as they are found.[23] Because of the separation of men from women and children upon their arrival to the camps and the security operations within al-Hol, ISIS

---

[20] It is important to note that much of the violence in the annex stems from the minority of hardened pro-ISIS women and, to a certain extent, their children. Nevertheless, camp guards have at times used violent force and instituted broad crackdowns to police the annex, as noted earlier. See Rights and Security International, 2021, p. 19.

[21] U.S. Department of Defense, Office of Inspector General, 2021b, p. 17.

[22] Similar concerns surrounding legal status, living conditions, security, and radicalization exist for the SDF-run prisons in northeastern Syria. The Al-Qa'ida in Iraq and the Islamic State of Iraq, ISIS's predecessor organizations, have a well-documented history of radicalizing prisoners and orchestrating prison breaks under U.S. military and Iraqi government control. However, we note only the similarities because further exploration remains outside the scope of this project. For more information, see Jessica D. Lewis, *Al-Qaeda in Iraq Resurgent: The Breaking the Walls Campaign, Part 1*, Washington, D.C.: Institute for the Study of War, Middle East Security Report 14, September 2013; Myriam Benraad, "Prisons in Iraq: A New Generation of Jihadists?" *CTC Sentinel*, Vol. 2, No. 12, December 2009.

[23] Examples include the detainment and placement into special camps of former Liberation Tigers of Tamil Eelam fighters in the Indian state of Tamil Nadu (sometimes followed by deportation to Sri Lanka) and the arrest of suspected Arakan Rohingya Salvation Army fighters in Bangladesh's Rohingya refugee camps. See Sreekumar Panicker Kodiyath and Sheethal Padathu Veettil, "Invisible People: Suspected LTTE Members in the Special Refugee Camps of Tamil Nadu," *Refugee Survey Quarterly*, Vol. 36, No. 1,

likely does not have a broad base of active fighters in al-Hol or Roj. However, because of previously mentioned limitations, we cannot accurately assess the extent of ISIS-affiliated membership within the camps. Anecdotal responses from interviews with AANES and NGO officials spanned the spectrum from noting limited to broad ISIS presence in the camps.[24]

Chapter Four highlighted outbreaks of violence between camp residents and guards, and there have been myriad instances of residents attacking and abusing each other. In some cases, disputes have broken out between residents over such issues as access to services or certain residents' ability to leave al-Hol while others remain restricted to the camp—issues that are a part of everyday life for residents.[25] However, there have been notable examples of violence in the foreigners' annex involving pro-ISIS women attacking other detainees who were less hardened in their support for the group. ISIS supporters espouse the group's ideology and police the annex, intimidating, beating, and, in egregious cases, killing women and children who do not comply. In one case, ISIS women enforcers reportedly strangled to death a 14-year-old Azerbaijani girl who had not, in their perspective, properly covered herself.[26] Violence involving pro-ISIS women in al-Hol's annex appears to go both ways. For instance, women in the foreigners' annex have also attacked pro-ISIS women whose husbands were reportedly part of the

---

2017; "'Several' Suspected Rohingya Insurgents in Custody: Bangladesh Official," *Radio Free Asia*, April 18, 2018.

[24] Of note, as foreign boys reach their teenage years, the SDF has separated some from their families in both al-Hol and Roj. Debate remains as to whether these teenaged boys are moved to AANES-administered prisons or to deradicalization centers, where they continue to lack freedom of movement. However, during the January 2022 siege of Ghuwayran Detention Facility, hundreds of teenage boys were used as human shields, and UNICEF reports at the time of the siege, up to 850 boys were held in the prison without any criminal charges. See Sancha, 2021; Heather Murdock, "The Children the World Left Behind," VOA, March 12, 2020; Katie Bo Williams, "Coalition Plans to Expand Giant ISIS Prison in Syria," *Defense One*, February 24, 2021; Henrietta Fore, "Children Caught Up in Al Hasakah Prison Violence Must Be Evacuated to Safety," UNICEF, January 25, 2022; Jane Arraf and Sangar Khaleel, "Teenage Inmates Found Among the 500 Dead in Syria Prison Attack," *New York Times*, January 31, 2022.

[25] Interview with NGO officials, phone, November 25, 2020.

[26] Rights and Security International, 2021, p. 18.

group's Amni, or intelligence service, and might have had a hand in ISIS's arrest or murder of the other women's husbands.[27]

External ISIS Members Support ISIS Propaganda and Violence in the Camps

Despite efforts by the AANES and SDF, women in the al-Hol foreigners' annex in particular have been able to maintain connections with ISIS members located outside the camp, leading to continued membership in and support for the group and their ability to receive financial support from ISIS.[28] This has allowed women to continue to recruit for ISIS within the camp as well. Given ISIS's persistent activity in the area, the U.S. Defense Intelligence Agency warned OIG that ISIS is trying to "reintegrate newly released detainees and ISIS-affiliated families from al-Hol into its ranks."[29] However, the U.S. Department of State reported to OIG that, through the end of 2020, it had not observed Syrian IDPs joining ISIS after the SDF released them from al-Hol, an assessment echoed by experts interviewed for this study.[30]

There is reason to be concerned about the presence of ISIS within Syria's IDP camps. Other cases indicate that such a presence is relatively common and can lead to security concerns and recruitment of displaced people into armed groups, as occurred among Afghan, Somali, and South Sudanese IDPs and refugees.[31] This activity exposes the displaced to a threat to their safety,

---

[27] Mironova, 2020.

[28] U.S. Department of Defense, Office of Inspector General, 2021b, p. 13.

[29] U.S. Department of Defense, Office of Inspector General, 2020c, p. 16.

[30] U.S. Department of Defense, Office of Inspector General, 2020c, p. 16; interview with a think tank researcher, phone, December 4, 2020; interview with NGO workers, phone, November 25, 2020.

[31] On Afghanistan, see European Asylum Support Office, *Country of Origin Information Report: Afghanistan Taliban Strategies—Recruitment*, Luxembourg, July 2012, pp. 20, 25, 30, 34, 37, 41–42; Ahmad Shuja Jamal, *The Fatemiyoun Army: Reintegration into Afghan Society*, Washington, D.C.: United States Institute of Peace, No. 443, March 2019, p. 5. On Somalia, see Letta Tayler and Chris Albin-Lackey, "Kenya Recruits Somali Refugees to Fight Islamists Back Home in Somalia," *Huffington Post*, March 18, 2010; Sudarsan Raghavan, "Somali Refugees Recruited to Fight Islamist Militia," *Washington*

as instead of being protected from violence, displaced persons are pulled back into the conflict by conflict participants entering camps. Additionally, recruiting the displaced from camps into an armed group or state force directly militarizes them and might in turn serve to legitimize an individual's views that violence is a legitimate option to use to achieve political goals.

Conversely, the greater risk of IDP recruitment and militarization might come not from ISIS, but from the SDF, which has actively recruited or conscripted able-bodied males into its security services. Some former IDPs might be willingly joining the SDF—enlisting in the Deir ez-Zor Military Council and other Sunni Arab elements—because it offers one of the scant opportunities for employment and salary in northeastern Syria. Indeed, one interviewee framed returning IDPs enlisting with the SDF as both a jobs and reintegration program because the AANES and SDF can offer "young men some form of employment or occupation while also keeping an eye on them" for security purposes and called it a "relatively secure approach," preferable to keeping the returning Syrian IDP population marginalized.[32] However, the SDF has also gang-pressed local males into military service, which has increased tensions between majority Sunni Arab communities in ar-Raqqah

---

Post, April 6, 2010; Karolina Eklöw and Florian Krampe, *Climate-Related Security Risks and Peacebuilding in Somalia*, Solna, Sweden: Stockholm International Peace Research Institute, No. 53, October 2019, pp. 20–21, 25; Matt Bryden, Arnaud Laloum, and Jörg Roofthooft, *Report of the Monitoring Group on Somalia Pursuant to Security Council Resolution 1853 (2008)*, New York: United Nations Security Council, S/2010/91, March 10, 2010, pp. 55–56; Human Rights Watch, "Kenya: Stop Recruitment of Somalis in Refugee Camps," October 22, 2009. For South Sudan, see Watchlist on Children and Armed Conflict, "South Sudan: Briefing Note for the UN Security Council Working Group on Children and Armed Conflict," February 2015, p. 2; Jonathan Kamoga, "South Sudan Rebels Recruiting Fighters in Ugandan Refugee Camps," *The Observer*, June 26, 2017.

[32] Interview with a think tank researcher, phone, December 4, 2020. Of note, for returning male IDPs enlisting with the SDF—particularly with the SDF's Syrian Arab Coalition wing, composed of Sunni Arab militias—the United States might be indirectly paying their salaries. Since at least FY 2017, the United States has provided stipends to the Syrian Arab Coalition through the Counter-ISIS Train and Equip Fund. See Office of the Secretary of Defense, *Justification for FY 2017 Overseas Contingency Operations (OCO) Syria Train & Equip Fund (STEF)*, Washington, D.C.: U.S. Department of Defense, February 2016, p. 4.

and Deir ez-Zor Province and the Kurdish-dominated SDF, presenting possible societal fissures that nefarious actors could exploit in the future.[33]

Despite their de facto detention, pro-ISIS women in al-Hol—and to a lesser extent in Roj—are able to maintain connections with ISIS members and supporters outside the camps. For instance, Mironova has observed an active online "marriage market" for ISIS-affiliated women in al-Hol who "marry" ISIS supporters—typically residing in Europe—who then help fund smuggling the women and their children out of al-Hol.[34] Additionally, the presence of ISIS leadership in al-Hol reflects the ability for members in Syria to maintain physical connections with group supporters in the camp. However, the majority of external connections are likely digital and facilitated by access to smartphones.[35] The policy challenges related to access to smartphones are addressed in the next section on smuggling. Another concern exists in addition to the women's ability to maintain access to ISIS members outside of the camps: Women who are simply trying to find a way out of al-Hol might end up being victims of human trafficking as well.

Smuggling Supports Continued Connections with ISIS

Smuggling of money, materials, weapons, and people into and out of the camp is also a major security concern in al-Hol because it can facilitate connection with ISIS cells outside the camp and increase the risk of violence within the camp. Smuggling reflects the permeability of the camp's security. As stated earlier, the SDF largely restricts foreign women and children to the annex and does not permit their freedom of movement in the camp, writ large. Nevertheless, because of al-Hol's large size and limited Asayesh and

---

[33] Dan Wilkofsky, "In Syria's Deir ez-Zor, SDF Conscription 'Severs Livelihoods,'" *Al-Monitor*, February 22, 2021; Human Rights Watch, "Syria: Armed Group Recruiting Children in Camps: People's Protection Units Enlist Under 18s from Vulnerable Families," August 3, 2018.

[34] Mironova, 2020.

[35] U.S. Department of Defense, Office of Inspector General, 2021a, p. 18; Mironova, 2020; interview with an academic, phone, November 20, 2020.

YPG force presence, the annex's security perimeter is porous and condu-
cive to smuggling. Mironova has reported that different modes of escaping
al-Hol—such as bribing a camp guard or paying a local worker to smug-
gle people out in water tanks—can cost more than $15,000 for a family.[36]
Indeed, OIG has reported that ISIS is able to move people and resources in
and out of the camp with relative ease. An estimated 200 foreigners escaped
al-Hol in 2020, despite DoD funding construction materials, generators,
lights, and security equipment (including cameras and biometric enrollment gear) to improve perimeter security.[37] In April 2021, the SDF detained
members of a suspected smuggling ring in al-Hol.[38] DoD has also worked
with the AANES and SDF to improve security at Roj.

ISIS often funds the smuggling of group loyalists out of the camps, com-
municating via cell phone.[39] However, smuggling out of Roj appears to be
significantly rarer compared with al-Hol. According to one expert interviewed in late 2020, only one woman had escaped Roj; in contrast, women
and children reportedly escaped al-Hol—often via smugglers—on a weekly
basis.[40] Roj's smaller size and more formal organization and administration
likely contribute to a more secure environment. However, the lower rate of
smuggling might also be, in part, because of camp guards' restrictions on

---

[36] Mironova, 2020; Lowcock noted in his statement to the United Nations Security
Council that amid Syria's economic crisis and the plummeting value of the Syrian
pound, the average household salary was 20 percent lower than average household
expenses. Smuggling payments significantly increase local guards and workers' salaries. See Mark Lowcock, Under-Secretary-General for Humanitarian Affairs and
Emergency Relief Coordinator, "Briefing to the Security Council on the Humanitarian
Situation in Syria," New York: United Nations Office for the Coordination of Humanitarian Affairs, February 25, 2021.

[37] U.S. Department of Defense, Office of Inspector General, 2019b, p. 9; Jeff Seldin,
"IS Winning Battle in Syria's Displaced-Persons Camps," VOA, February 13, 2021; U.S.
Department of Defense, Office of Inspector General, *Operation Inherent Resolve: Lead
Inspector General Report to the United States Congress*, Alexandria, Va., April 1, 2020–
June 30, 2020b, p. 5; U.S. Department of Defense, Office of Inspector General, 2019a, p. 25.

[38] U.S. Department of Defense, Office of Inspector General, 2021b, p. 66.

[39] Mironova, 2020.

[40] Interview with a think tank researcher, November 12, 2020; Mironova, 2020.

access to phones, which restricts the women's ability to communicate with smugglers and outside ISIS members.[41]

Multiple experts interviewed for this study stated that limiting access to cell phones might be an effective means of cutting down on smuggling and escapes from the annex, while also inhibiting communication with outside ISIS elements. Restricting phone access for women and children in the annex would also cut them off from their families and the outside world, which provide many with mental escapes and moderating influences, potentially increasing insularity and potential for radicalization among women in al-Hol and Roj.[42] Regardless, to bolster camp security, the SDF has periodically attempted to confiscate phones and conducted biometric registration efforts to build an electronic database of suspected ISIS members and supporters within the camp.[43]

The experts we interviewed caveated that such measures would not eliminate leakage from the camp altogether. Moreover, such a policy could lead to blowback from the international community, who could characterize the policy as unnecessary, cruel, and ineffective, as occurred when Bangladesh instituted its telecommunications restrictions on Burmese Rohingya refugee camps.[44] In 2019 to 2020, Bangladeshi authorities claimed that restricting telecommunications and internet access was done to improve the security situation.[45] However, criminal and militant activity inside the camps

---

[41] Interview with a think tank researcher, Washington, D.C., November 11, 2020. Mironova reported that, as of July 2020, only one person had escaped Roj, and the smuggling cost was approximately $40,000. The significantly higher cost of smuggling out of Roj compared with al-Hol might reflect a relative disparity in the two camps' levels of security. See Mironova, 2020.

[42] Interview with an academic, Washington, D.C., November 12, 2020; interview with an academic, phone, November 20, 2020.

[43] U.S. Department of Defense, Office of Inspector General, 2020b, p. 5; U.S. Department of Defense, Office of Inspector General, 2019a, p. 25.

[44] Human Rights Watch, "Bangladesh: Internet Ban Risks Rohingya Lives," March 26, 2020; Human Rights Watch, "Bangladesh: Internet Blackout on Rohingya Refugees," September 13, 2019b.

[45] Hannah Beech, "A Million Refugees May Soon Lose Their Line to the Outside World," *New York Times*, September 5, 2019; Human Rights Watch, 2020; Human Rights Watch, "Bangladesh: Clampdown on Rohingya Refugees," September 7, 2019a.

continued despite the restriction on internet and telecommunication access, indicating that such a strategy might not prevent these activities from occurring.[46] Furthermore, aid workers "reported that the shutdown . . . hampered their ability to provide assistance, including responding to emergencies."[47]

Restricted Freedom of Movement Is a Blunt Tactic, Affecting All Residents

Freedom of movement outside al-Hol and Roj is highly restricted, especially for foreign populations. In al-Hol, foreigners are not even allowed to exit the foreigners' annex to shop at the camp's markets unless under armed Asayesh supervision. Often, government policies, especially those that isolate displaced persons physically and/or economically or impede their ability to integrate into local communities (as most often seen for refugees in host countries), exacerbate the disenfranchisement of displaced persons, making them more vulnerable to recruitment and/or radicalization by armed groups. Indeed, past research has indicated that radicalization might occur in instances where an individual feels isolated from their community or is forced or voluntarily chooses to live separately from other segments of society.[48] This isolation might take the form of "segregation and enclavization" where communities are settled and separated and, in turn, might find themselves rejecting both their local community and their host.[49] In this situation, radicalization "appears to grow out of feelings of fear and isolation that ostracism from a society or a group causes."[50] These feelings of separation might in turn increase the success rate of extremist recruiters

---

[46] Amnesty International, 2020.

[47] Human Rights Watch, 2019b.

[48] Marina Eleftheriadou, "Refugee Radicalization/Militarization in the Age of the European Refugee Crisis: A Composite Model," *Terrorism and Political Violence,* Vol. 32, No. 8, 2020; Sude, 2020.

[49] Eleftheriadou, 2020.

[50] Eleftheriadou, 2020.

seeking to draw potential fighters into the ranks of an armed group.[51] As emphasized elsewhere in this report, it does not appear that the displaced are more likely to be radicalized or turn to militancy than the general population. However, creating spaces allowing displaced communities to be able to settle and join the general population might allow individuals to find a place for themselves and deter feelings of separation from the community.

Summary

Limited resources to maintain security in the camps lead not only to an increasingly insecure environment in which displaced persons must live but also to complications in providing necessary humanitarian resources. Moreover, the insecurity decreases the ability for security forces and NGOs to gain an accurate understanding of the risks and threats present in the camps, especially as collective punishment efforts are used to bring the most extreme elements with ISIS affiliation under control. There is no doubt that there are camp inhabitants living in al-Hol and Roj who still believe in ISIS ideology and have interests in expanding the group's membership. However, more research is necessary to fully understand the scope and reach of these ISIS adherents in the camps, both in al-Hol's foreigners' annex and the main camp. **An independent assessment of the extent of radicalization within the camps and the external ISIS network, including connections to camp inhabitants, is required to understand the scope of the problem**.

Exposure to discrimination, corruption, or abuse by security forces—defined as *elements of injustice* in a 2015 study from Mercy Corps—are also drivers of radicalization. Moreover, the study did not find a direct relationship between living in poverty or being unemployed and being more vulnerable to radicalization.[52] It is not the only recent study drawing connections

---

[51] Yvonne Jazz Rowa, "Disruptive Islamism: 'Islamic Radicalisation' in Public Discourse, and the Strategies and Impact of Terrorist Communication on Refugees and Host Communities," *Behavioral Sciences of Terrorism and Political Aggression*, January 29, 2021.

[52] Mercy Corps, *Youth and Consequences: Unemployment, Injustice and Violence*, Portland, Oreg., 2015.

to systemic injustices, often the result of government policies.[53] The three "durable solutions" for refugees—returning home, resettlement to third countries (such as the United States or European Union), or integration into the host country—occur at low rates, forcing displaced persons to remain in the camps for indeterminant periods of time.[54] **Identifying ways to increase freedom of movement of camp residents and provide economic opportunities to decrease the reliance on smuggling within the camps is necessary.** The fact that northeastern Syria and the camps are run by the AANES instead of the Syrian government further compounds and complicates policy options and decisions. Even with the international support it has received, the AANES has a limited number of resources and options to address the challenges in the region, in particular when related to integrating camp residents with the local environment. **The Counter-ISIS Coalition's initiatives to increase funding, training, and related resources to support SDF efforts to maintain security internal to al-Hol and Roj and in the surrounding areas in northeastern Syria are a start but are not sufficient to challenge ISIS activity. More resources and expertise from the Counter-ISIS Coalition, the United Nations, NGOs, and the European Union are required to support the AANES and SDF.**

---

[53] The Soufan Center, *The Nexus Between Human Security and Preventing/Countering Violent Extremism: Case Studies from Bosnia and Herzegovina, Niger, and Tunisia*, New York, March 2020.

[54] U.S. Department of State, Bureau of Population, Refugees, and Migration, "Durable Solutions," webpage, undated.

CHAPTER SIX

Conclusions

The U.S.-led military campaign to oust ISIS from its strongholds in northeastern Syria resulted in mass displacement and has stretched AANES and SDF authorities' ability to care for and secure the displaced populations to the breaking point. Above all else, the situations in al-Hol and Roj present monumental humanitarian challenges requiring substantial international attention to mitigate the hardships and human suffering in the camps, in particular for the approximately 40,000 children and youth who are likely traumatized and lack opportunities to easily improve their futures. Al-Hol and Roj also present a significant security concern, given the camp residents' vulnerability to exploitation by armed groups and the likely criminal history of at least some of the residents. Table 6.1 provides an overview of our strategic and tactical recommendations for addressing these challenges.

The Islamic State might be territorially defeated, but the group remains active and lethal, and it is almost certainly seeking to extend its influence and undertake recruitment in the camps—especially among the detained population of foreign women and adolescents. **Repatriating and resettling the camps' residents—which would alleviate pressure on the AANES, SDF, and NGOs servicing the camps—has proceeded slowly and sporadically, largely because of home countries' decisions to not do so out of concern that their own justice systems might be inadequate to the challenge**. Indefinite inaction on al-Hol and Roj is not a solution to the incipient crisis mounting in northeastern Syria. Humanitarian and security conditions will likely remain tenuous and could deteriorate further, as tens of thousands of women and children languish in miserable, dangerous environments.

The most difficult task will be determining the extent to which camp inhabitants are indeed radicalized or sympathetic to ISIS. The assumption, particularly for foreign families, is that many continue to be affiliated

TABLE 6.1

Recommendations

Category of Recommendation	Strategic Recommendation	Tactical Recommendation
Policy	• Repatriate camp residents. • Support the Iraqi government, the AANES, and the Syrian peace process to stabilize Iraq and Syria to facilitate the return of camp residents to their homes. • Reassess asylum and refugee processes in Western countries to facilitate increased resettlement of those who cannot return to their homes because of discrimination. • Conduct an independent assessment of the extent of radicalization within the camps and connections with the external ISIS network to understand the scope of the problem.	• Develop a process to determine the legal status of the foreigners and increase repatriation to their home countries. • Develop and resource judicial systems in the AANES to investigate, collect evidence, and try suspected ISIS affiliates. • Establish assessment structures and processes to determine safe paths for adolescent boys in the camps.
Humanitarian services	• Increase funding and resources for WASH, living structures, and physical and mental health services. • Provide increased funding to and appropriate security support for NGOs providing services within the camps to improve services.	• Establish an international fund with mandatory contributions by nations with citizens currently in the camps. • Increase integration and freedom of movement between the camps and local communities to provide economic opportunities to residents.
Security	• Increase funding, training, and resources for security forces.	• Increase force size, provide training for policing, and provide equipment such as appropriate fencing to prevent smuggling. • Consider separating and isolating the most radicalized foreigners from the general population, following the appropriate security assessment.

with ISIS or desire to be and hence are a significant security risk for their local communities. The legal and policy debates surrounding repatriation decisions, judicial processes, improvement of living conditions within the camps, and security operations and conditions in the camps are all affected by this assumption. Indeed, there is a group of inhabitants at al-Hol and potentially Roj who remain sympathetic to ISIS, but we could not determine the spread of their influence with our foundational research. **Determining ISIS's influence within the camps is necessary to inform future decisions**.

Ultimately, it will be critical to return the camps' residents back to their homes and villages in Syria and Iraq and, in the case of the foreign contingent, back to their home countries. Progress is being made with respect to enabling the Syrian residents to leave the camps, though efforts will need to take care that individuals do not find themselves being recruited by remaining ISIS cells or overly influenced to join the SDF. The Iraqi government likewise confronts the challenge of bringing its citizens in al-Hol home. In the absence of being able to identify who is and is not affiliated with or radicalized by ISIS, Iraqi officials have opted to keep Iraqi citizens living in Syrian refugee camps rather than risking a domestic security incident, increasing the burden on the already stressed judicial system, or upsetting Iraqis with additional domestic displaced persons camps.

The most difficult legal and policy challenges relate to repatriating foreign families. A litany of policy reports has urged the international community—in particular, Canada, the United Kingdom, France, and Denmark—to depopulate al-Hol's foreigners' annex and return their citizens home. Our report did not assess the specific contingencies affecting each of these countries, though the political and security risk to taking back people who have presumably been affiliated with ISIS at least at some point is seemingly obvious. In the absence of an ability to collect evidence against and successfully prosecute individuals with presumed ISIS ties and provide long prison sentences, such individuals, if so radicalized, could potentially launch domestic terrorist attacks. However, keeping such individuals detained without trial for an indeterminant period of time under poor humanitarian and security conditions only increases the likelihood that the women and children will constitute their own security risk. Further delays will only increase the challenge of repatriation. For these reasons and the moral necessity to not let the innocent children of the foreign ISIS fighters and their wives continue to live in poor humanitarian and security conditions, **we urge the international community to redouble efforts to bring their citizens home**.

To assist repatriation efforts, the United States and allied countries should continue to apply diplomatic pressure to motivate repatriation and should work to provide technical assistance as needed to help foreign governments and Kurdish authorities do so in a secure and politically feasible manner. One critical ingredient is to **help national and regional governments in these countries, including the AANES and SDF, collect evidence on ISIS involvement** that would facilitate prosecution and successful imprisonment. One civil society organization, for example, has worked with foreign detainees to help them tell their stories, which might aid in their return home. It might also be possible for Western European law enforcement and intelligence services to better identify the radicalization status of the foreign families in al-Hol and Roj. However, funding, resources, and cooperation with the AANES and SDF would be required, along with support from international NGOs to ensure that people's rights, enshrined in international humanitarian law, are not violated.

Another critical issue relates to the legal status of foreign families. As we note in both the introduction and Chapter Two, Iraqi residents of al-Hol and Roj are given the legal designation of *refugees,* while the Syrian residents are deemed *IDPs.* These designations afford certain legal protections and humanitarian status to these individuals. In contrast, foreign families reside in a state of limbo, not qualifying for refugee or IDP status. And, in some instances, European countries have stripped these women of citizenship or denied their children of birthright citizenship, further placing them and their children in legal limbo. In addition, although for all practical purposes they exist in a state of detention, they are not legally categorized as *detainees.* This lack of specificity with regard to their status contributes to foreign governments choosing to leave their citizens in the camps without providing legal pathways to depart northeastern Syria. Consequently, **developing a process to determine the legal status of the foreigners and developing and supporting a justice system to try suspected ISIS affiliates is critical for ultimately providing legal imprisonment sentences or reintegrating camp residents into society.**

Finally, **until camp residents can be returned to their home communities or nations, it will be critical to ensure proper humanitarian and**

security conditions in the camps. As we noted in Chapter Four, al-Hol and Roj suffer significant challenges with regard to humanitarian conditions. An insufficient number of medical staff and poor WASH services reportedly contribute to disease outbreaks. Educational services are also limited, and there is a significant unmet need for mental health care. Addressing these needs presents a pressing humanitarian requirement, while not improving them risks inflaming attitudes against the AANES, SDF, and international community, which could provide opportunities for ISIS recruitment. Finally, provisioning such services, especially education and mental health care, along with other forms of psychosocial services, such as religious counseling, might provide an opportunity for camp residents to not only avoid extremism but also desist, disengage, and deradicalize. Consequently, at a minimum, **we urge the Counter-ISIS Coalition, the United Nations, and the European Union to dedicate greater financial and physical resources to these camps to improve the quality of living conditions and humanitarian services—including medical and educational services**. Specifically, we recommend **the establishment of an international fund with mandatory contributions by nations that have citizens currently in the camps or prisons**.

The poor security situation contributes to the inability of Kurdish authorities and NGOs to consistently provide humanitarian services and maintain stability within the camps, further isolating residents from local societies. As we noted in Chapter Five, al-Hol and Roj suffer from limited security service presence and oversight. The implications of a shortage of security personnel are acutely seen in the foreign annexes, where violent security incidents are not uncommon and some residents face intimidation and threats from more-extreme members. Smuggling and overt instances of ISIS influence are also present. **Addressing these security issues will be critical, and it will require, at a minimum, more resources dedicated to the camps to increase the size of the camp security force and increase resources and training available to them**. It also seems that improvements in security policies and posture will be necessary to limit the influence of radicalized families in the foreign annex. Our research team was unable to visit the camps directly, and so it is hard to offer unique insights on specific security policies, although others have recommended such changes as restricting cell phone usage, biometrically enrolling inhabitants, conducting regular security sweeps in the camps, and improving coalition training of the SDF. There might also be value in separating more-radicalized members from those who are not radicalized or exposing those who no longer wish to be affiliated with the Islamic State to those who have not been radicalized by the group. Initial efforts at Roj to move foreign women to the general population and away from more-extremist elements have shown positive results.

Ultimately, our tactical recommendations to improve the current humanitarian and security conditions at al-Hol and Roj would, if implemented, reinforce efforts to repatriate camp residents and vice versa. Improving the living conditions, increasing access to employment, and expanding security can reduce the vulnerability of residents to ISIS's influence. These near-term improvements can provide AANES and SDF authorities, along with foreign governments, the space to improve justice processes to facilitate repatriation, which, in the long term, reduces opportunities for ISIS to radicalize camp inhabitants. Reviews of long-term displacement from the past three decades highlight that ignoring the situation or providing the bare minimum of resources does not lead to the closure of camps or reduce the vulnerability of residents to radicalization. Strategic decisions are required to fulfill the moral and ethical responsibilities to displaced persons and reduce continuation of violence in the future.

Abbreviations

AANES	Autonomous Administration of North and East Syria
COVID-19	coronavirus disease 2019
DoD	U.S. Department of Defense
DoS	U.S. Department of State
FY	fiscal year
ICRC	International Committee of the Red Cross
IDP	internally displaced person
ISIS	Islamic State of Iraq and Syria
NGO	nongovernmental organization
OIG	Office of Inspector General
SDF	Syrian Democratic Forces
UNHCR	United Nations High Commissioner for Refugees
WASH	water, sanitation, and hygiene
YPG	People's Protection Units (Yekîneyên Parastina Gel)

References

Abboud, Samer, "The Siege of Nahr al-Bared and the Palestinian Refugees in Lebanon," *Arab Studies Quarterly*, Vol. 31, No. 1–2, Winter–Spring 2009, pp. 31–48.

Abdul-Wahid, Farid, and Samya Kullab, "100 Iraqi Families from IS-Linked Camp in Syria Repatriated," *Washington Post*, May 25, 2021.

"Ain Issa . . . From a Cotton Factory to a Camp of Thousands of IDPs" ["عين عيسى . . . من مستودع أقطان إلى مخيم آلاف النازحين"], *Asharq Al-Awsat*, October 13, 2019.

Al-Khalidi, Suleiman, "The Cost of Ten Years of Devastating War in Syria," Reuters, May 26, 2021.

Al Khateeb, Firas, "Returning Iraqis Face Dire Conditions Following Camp Closures," UNHCR, May 27, 2021.

Amnesty International, "Sri Lanka: Armed Groups Infiltrating Refugee Camps," press release, London, March 14, 2007.

———, "Afghanistan's Refugees: Forty Years of Dispossession," June 20, 2019.

———, "Bangladesh: Rohingya Refugees' Safety Must Be Ensured Amid Violent Clashes in Cox's Bazaar," press release, October 9, 2020.

"Are Militants Tightening Grip on Rohingya Refugee Camps?" Deutsche Welle, September 24, 2019.

Arraf, Jane, and Sangar Khaleel, "Teenage Inmates Found Among the 500 Dead in Syria Prison Attack," *New York Times*, January 31, 2022.

Atkinson, Kelly E., "Refugees and Recruitment: Understanding Violations Against Children in Armed Conflict with Novel Data," *Journal of Peacebuilding and Development*, Vol. 15, No. 1, 2020, pp. 75–90.

Awad, Monica, "Iraqi Families Flee Mosul, Seeking Refuge Across the Syrian Border," UNICEF, November 7, 2016.

Awad, Monica, and Delil Soulieman, "Child-Friendly Spaces Offer Respite for Raqqa's Displaced Children," UNICEF, August 23, 2017.

Aziz, Ammar, "Work to Build Umla Camp for 'ISIS Families' Resumed," *Kirkuk Now*, October 22, 2020.

Bader, Laetitia, and Ben Rawlence, *Hostages of the Gatekeepers: Abuses Against Internally Displaced in Mogadishu, Somalia*, Human Rights Watch, March 2013.

Baffa, Richard C., Nathan Vest, Wing Yi Chan, and Abby Fanlo, *Defining and Understanding the Next Generation of Salafi-Jihadis*, Santa Monica, Calif.: RAND Corporation, PE-341-ODNI, 2019. As of March 5, 2021: https://www.rand.org/pubs/perspectives/PE341.html

Bahar, Dany, and Meagan Dooley, "No Refugees and Migrants Left Behind," in Homi Kharas, John W. McArthur, and Izumi Ohno, eds., *Leave No One Behind: Time for Specifics on the Sustainable Development Goals*, Washington, D.C.: Brookings Institution Press, 2019, pp. 79–104.

Barbarani, Sofia, "Leaving Syria's Notorious al-Hol Camp, Civilians Find Little to Go Home to," *New Humanitarian*, January 14, 2021.

Beech, Hannah, "A Million Refugees May Soon Lose Their Line to the Outside World," *New York Times*, September 5, 2019.

Benraad, Myriam, "Prisons in Iraq: A New Generation of Jihadists?" *CTC Sentinel*, Vol. 2, No. 12, December 2009, pp. 16–18.

Bird, Lyndsay, *Surviving School: Education for Refugee Children from Rwanda 1994–1996*, Paris: International Institute for Educational Planning, 2003.

Blue, Victor J., "After the 'War of Annihilation' Against ISIS," *Time*, April 6, 2019.

Bryden, Matt, Arnaud Laloum, and Jörg Roofthooft, *Report of the Monitoring Group on Somalia Pursuant to Security Council Resolution 1853 (2008)*, New York: United Nations Security Council, S/2010/91, March 10, 2010.

Chaaban, Jad, Nisreen Salti, Hala Ghattas, Alexandra Irani, Tala Ismail, and Lara Batlouni, *Survey on the Socioeconomic Status of Palestine Refugees in Lebanon 2015*, American University of Beirut and the United Nations Relief and Works Agency for Palestine Refugees in the Near East, 2016.

Christien, Agathe, Emma Jouenne, and Elena Scott-Kakures, "How COVID-19 Underscores the Urgent Need to Repatriate Women and Children from Northeast Syria Camps," Georgetown Institute for Women, Peace and Security, December 9, 2020.

Combined Joint Task Force–Operation Inherent Resolve, "Syrian Democratic Forces Liberate Raqqa," news release, U.S. Department of Defense, October 20, 2017.

Culbertson, Shelly, "The Urgent Need for an Education Plan in Mosul," *RAND Blog*, March 27, 2017. As of August 6, 2021: https://www.rand.org/blog/2017/03/the-urgent-need-for-an-education-plan-in-mosul.html

Culbertson, Shelly, and Louay Constant, *Education of Syrian Refugee Children: Managing the Crisis in Turkey, Lebanon, and Jordan*, Santa Monica, Calif.: RAND Corporation, RR-859-CMEPP, 2015. As of May 27, 2021: https://www.rand.org/pubs/research_reports/RR859.html

Culbertson, Shelly, Tom Ling, Marie-Louise Henham, Jennie Corbett, Rita T. Karam, Paulina Pankowska, Catherine L. Saunders, Jacopo Bellasio, and Ben Baruch, *Evaluation of the Emergency Education Response for Syrian Refugee Children and Host Communities in Jordan*, Santa Monica, Calif.: RAND Corporation, RR-1203-UNICF, 2016. As of May 27, 2021: https://www.rand.org/pubs/research_reports/RR1203.html

Dalgaard-Nielsen, Anja, "Violent Radicalization in Europe: What We Know and What We Do Not Know," *Studies in Conflict and Terrorism*, Vol. 33, No. 9, 2010, pp. 797–814.

Demirjian, Karoun, "Raids on ISIS Camp in Syria Yield Hundreds of Arrests," *Washington Post*, September 7, 2022.

Directorate-General for Migration and Home Affairs, European Commission, "Prevention of Radicalisation," webpage, undated. As of April 9, 2021: https://ec.europa.eu/home-affairs/what-we-do/policies/counter-terrorism/radicalisation_en

Eklöw, Karolina, and Florian Krampe, *Climate-Related Security Risks and Peacebuilding in Somalia*, Solna, Sweden: Stockholm International Peace Research Institute, No. 53, October 2019.

Eleftheriadou, Marina, "Refugee Radicalization/Militarization in the Age of the European Refugee Crisis: A Composite Model," *Terrorism and Political Violence,* Vol. 32, No. 8, 2020, pp. 1797–1818.

European Asylum Support Office, *Country of Origin Information Report: Afghanistan Taliban Strategies—Recruitment*, Luxembourg, July 2012.

———, "Deir Ez-Zor," webpage, September 2020. As of May 14, 2021: https://easo.europa.eu/country-guidance-syria/deir-ez-zor

Fore, Henrietta, "Children Caught Up in Al Hasakah Prison Violence Must Be Evacuated to Safety," UNICEF, January 25, 2022.

Haer, Roos, and Tobias Hecker, "Recruiting Refugees for Militarization: The Determinants of Mobilization Attempts," *Journal of Refugee Studies*, Vol. 32, No. 1, 2019, pp. 1–22.

Hamasaeed, Sarhang, "What Will Become of Iraqis in Al-Hol?" United States Institute of Peace, November 19, 2020.

Hardan, Mohammed, "How Islamic State Returned to Haunt Civilians in Northeast Syria," *Al-Monitor*, February 22, 2021.

Hassan, Lila, "Repatriating ISIS Foreign Fighters Is Key to Stemming Radicalization, Experts Say, but Many Countries Don't Want Their Citizens Back," *Frontline*, April 6, 2021.

Horowitz, Jonathan, "Kurdish-Held Detainees in Syria Are Not in a 'Legal Gray Area,'" *Just Security*, April 13, 2018.

Houry, Nadim, "Bringing ISIS to Justice: Running Out of Time?" Human Rights Watch, February 5, 2019.

Hubbard, Ben, and Constant Méheut, "Western Countries Leave Children of ISIS in Syrian Camps," *New York Times*, May 31, 2020.

Hujale, Moulid, "The Refugee Camp That Became a City," *New Humanitarian*, January 20, 2016.

Human Rights Watch, "Kenya: Stop Recruitment of Somalis in Refugee Camps," October 22, 2009.

———, "Syria: Armed Group Recruiting Children in Camps: People's Protection Units Enlist Under 18s from Vulnerable Families," August 3, 2018.

———, "Bangladesh: Clampdown on Rohingya Refugees," September 7, 2019a.

———, "Bangladesh: Internet Blackout on Rohingya Refugees," September 13, 2019b.

———, "Bangladesh: Internet Ban Risks Rohingya Lives," March 26, 2020.

———, "Thousands of Foreigners Unlawfully Held in NE Syria," March 23, 2021.

"Hundreds Linked to IS Transfered from Syria to Iraq," *Defense Post*, October 19, 2022.

Hurley, Julia C., "Coronavirus and ISIS: The Challenge of Repatriation from Al-Hol," United States Institute of Peace, May 28, 2020.

International Committee of the Red Cross, "Detainees," webpage, undated a. As of August 25, 2021:
https://casebook.icrc.org/glossary/detainees

———, "Detention," webpage, undated b. As of May 14, 2021:
https://casebook.icrc.org/glossary/detention

———, *Internally Displaced Persons and International Humanitarian Law*, Geneva, Switzerland, December 2017.

International Crisis Group, *Nurturing Instability: Lebanon's Palestinian Refugee Camps*, Middle East Report No. 84, Brussels, February 19, 2009.

———, *Women and Children First: Repatriating the Westerners Affiliated with ISIS*, Middle East Report No. 208, Brussels, November 18, 2019.

———, *Exiles in Their Own Country: Dealing with Displacement in Post-ISIS Iraq*, Crisis Group Middle East Briefing No. 79, Brussels, October 19, 2020.

International Organization for Migration, "Displacement Tracking Matrix: Iraq Mission," webpage, February 28, 2021. As of March 23, 2021:
http://iraqdtm.iom.int/

International Rescue Committee, "Data Analyzed by the IRC Reveals Staggering Health and Humanitarian Needs of Children in Al Hol Camp, Northeast Syria—Urging Repatriation of Foreign Children," press release, al-Hol, Syria, September 16, 2019.

———, "NE Syria: 60% Increase in COVID-19 Cases in Past Week, IRC Calls for Increased Health Capacity," press release, New York, August 17, 2020.

Jamal, Ahmad Shuja, *The Fatemiyoun Army: Reintegration into Afghan Society*, Washington, D.C.: United States Institute of Peace, No. 443, March 2019.

Jenkins, Brian Michael, "Options for Dealing with Islamic State Foreign Fighters Currently Detained in Syria," *CTC Sentinel*, Vol. 12, No. 5, May–June 2019, pp. 11–23.

Joshi, Paramjit T., and Deborah A. O'Donnell, "Consequences of Child Exposure to War and Terrorism," *Clinical Child and Family Psychology Review*, Vol. 6, No. 4, December 2003, pp. 275–292.

Kamoga, Jonathan, "South Sudan Rebels Recruiting Fighters in Ugandan Refugee Camps," *The Observer*, June 26, 2017.

"Killings on the Rise in Syria's al-Hol Camp," *Al-Monitor*, February 18, 2021.

Kittleson, Shelly, "Iraq Suspends Repatriations from Syria's Notorious Islamic State Camp al-Hol," *Al-Monitor*, November 8, 2022.

Kodiyath, Sreekumar Panicker, and Sheethal Padathu Veettil, "Invisible People: Suspected LTTE Members in the Special Refugee Camps of Tamil Nadu," *Refugee Survey Quarterly*, Vol. 36, No. 1, 2017, pp. 126–145.

Kullab, Samya, "Camp Closures Force Iraqi Families Back to Shattered Homes," Associated Press, December 16, 2020.

The Kurdish Project, "YPG: People's Protection Units," webpage, undated. As of May 14, 2021:
https://thekurdishproject.org/history-and-culture/kurdish-nationalism/peoples-protection-units-ypg/

Kuznar, Lawrence, Ali Jafri, and Eric Kuznar, *Dealing with Radicalization in IDP Camps*, Boston, Mass.: NSI, February 2020.

Lakhani, Sadaf, and Rahmatullah Amiri, *Displacement and the Vulnerability to Mobilize for Violence: Evidence from Afghanistan*, Washington, D.C.: United States Institute of Peace, No. 155, January 2020.

Lamb, Robert D., and Brooke Shawn, *Political Governance and Strategy in Afghanistan*, Washington, D.C.: Center for Strategic and International Studies, April 2012.

Lewis, Jessica D., *Al-Qaeda in Iraq Resurgent: The Breaking the Walls Campaign, Part 1*, Washington, D.C.: Institute for the Study of War, Middle East Security Report 14, September 2013.

Lischer, Sarah Kanyon, *Dangerous Sanctuaries: Refugee Camps, Civil War, and the Dilemmas of Humanitarian Aid*, Ithaca, N.Y.: Cornell University Press, 2005.

Lopez, C. Todd, "DoD to Fund Better Detention Facilities in Syria, But Best Solution Is Detainee Repatriation," DoD News, July 14, 2022.

Loveluck, Louisa, "In Syrian Camp for Women and Children Who Left ISIS Caliphate, a Struggle Even to Register Names," *Washington Post*, June 28, 2020.

Loveluck, Louisa, and Sarah Cahlan, "Prison Break: ISIS Fighters Launched a Brazen Attack to Free Their Comrades," *Washington Post*, February 3, 2022.

Loveluck, Louisa, Souad Mekhennet, Loveday Morris, and Alice Martins, "Castaways from the Islamic State," *Washington Post*, December 24, 2019.

Loveluck, Louisa, and Mustafa Salim, "Iraq Is Pushing to Build an Isolation Camp for 30,000 Iraqis Who Lived Under ISIS in Syria," *Washington Post*, May 2, 2019.

———, "Iraq Wants Thousands Displaced by the ISIS War to Go Home. They May Be Killed if They Do," *Washington Post*, December 22, 2020.

Lowcock, Mark, Under-Secretary-General for Humanitarian Affairs and Emergency Relief Coordinator, "Briefing to the Security Council on the Humanitarian Situation in Syria," New York: United Nations Office for the Coordination of Humanitarian Affairs, February 25, 2021.

McKay, Gillian, and Melissa Parker, "Epidemics," in Tim Allen, Anna Macdonald, and Henry Radice, eds., *Humanitarianism: A Dictionary of Concepts*, New York: Routledge, 2018, pp. 82–83.

McKenzie, David, and Brent Swails, "Sanctuary Without End: The Refugees the World Forgot," CNN, October 2015.

Médecins Sans Frontières, "'In Al-Hol Camp, Almost No Healthcare Is Available,'" August 27, 2020.

———, "A Decade of War in Syria: 10 Years of Increasing Humanitarian Needs," March 3, 2021.

Mednick, Sam, "Inside the Troubled Repatriation of Iraqis from Syria's Al-Hol Camp," *New Humanitarian*, June 7, 2021.

Mercy Corps, *Youth and Consequences: Unemployment, Injustice and Violence*, Portland, Oreg., 2015.

Mironova, Vera, "Life Inside Syria's al-Hol Camp," Middle East Institute, July 9, 2020.

Mogelson, Luke, "America's Abandonment of Syria," *New Yorker*, April 20, 2020.

Mumin, Abdalle Ahmed, "Somalia's Displacement Camp 'Gatekeepers'— 'Parasites' or Aid Partners?" *New Humanitarian*, July 18, 2019.

Murdock, Heather, "The Children the World Left Behind," VOA, March 12, 2020.

Nicholson, Frances, *The Right to Family Life and Family Unity of Refugees and Others in Need of International Protection and the Family Definition Applied*, 2nd ed., Geneva, Switzerland: United Nations High Commissioner for Refugees, January 2018.

Norwegian Ministry of Justice and Public Security, *Action Plan Against Radicalisation and Violent Extremism*, Oslo, August 28, 2014.

Norwegian Refugee Council, *Supporting Kakuma's Refugees: The Importance of Freedom of Movement*, Oslo, August 2018.

Office of the Secretary of Defense, *Justification for FY 2017 Overseas Contingency Operations (OCO) Syria Train & Equip Fund (STEF)*, Washington, D.C.: U.S. Department of Defense, February 2016.

Office of the United Nations High Commissioner for Human Rights, "The Principle of *Non-Refoulement* Under International Human Rights Law," undated.

Raghavan, Sudarsan, "Somali Refugees Recruited to Fight Islamist Militia," *Washington Post*, April 6, 2010.

REACH, "Camp Profile: Mahmoudli," fact sheet, February 2020a.

———, "Camp Profile: Abu Khashab," fact sheet, July 2020b.

———, "Camp Profile: Areesheh," fact sheet, September 2020c.

———, "Camp Profile: Al Hol," fact sheet, October 2020d.

———, "Camp Profile: Roj," fact sheet, October 2020e.

Reid, Kathryn, "Syrian Refugee Crisis: Facts, FAQs, and How to Help," World Vision, March 11, 2021.

Rights and Security International, *Europe's Guantanamo: The Indefinite Detention of European Women and Children in North East Syria*, Version 2, London, February 17, 2021.

Robinson, Eric, Daniel Egel, Patrick B. Johnston, Sean Mann, Alexander D. Rothenberg, and David Stebbins, *When the Islamic State Comes to Town: The Economic Impact of Islamic State Governance in Iraq and Syria*, Santa Monica, Calif.: RAND Corporation, RR-1970-RC, 2017. As of May 14, 2021: https://www.rand.org/pubs/research_reports/RR1970.html

Rosenblatt, Nate, and David Kilcullen, *How Raqqa Became the Capital of ISIS*, Washington, D.C.: New America, July 2019.

Rowa, Yvonne Jazz, "Disruptive Islamism: 'Islamic Radicalisation' in Public Discourse, and the Strategies and Impact of Terrorist Communication on Refugees and Host Communities," *Behavioral Sciences of Terrorism and Political Aggression,* January 29, 2021.

Said, Rodi, "Islamic State 'Caliphate' Defeated, Yet Threat Persists," Reuters, March 23, 2019.

Saieh, Alexandra, and Naomi Petersohn, *Paperless People of Post-Conflict Iraq: Denied Rights, Barred from Basic Services and Excluded from Reconstruction Efforts,* Oslo: Norwegian Refugee Council, September 16, 2019.

Salehyan, Idean, "Transnational Rebels: Neighboring States as Sanctuary for Rebel Groups," *World Politics,* Vol. 59, No. 2, 2007, pp. 217–242.

Sancha, Natalia, "The Transformation of ISIS Women in Syria's Al Roj Camp," *El País,* March 26, 2021.

Save the Children, *Rewrite the Future: Education for Children in Conflict-Affected Countries,* London, 2006.

———, "Repatriation of Foreign Children in Syria Slowed by COVID-19, as New Footage Emerges of Life in Camps," February 1, 2021.

Seldin, Jeff, "IS Winning Battle in Syria's Displaced-Persons Camps," VOA, February 13, 2021.

"'Several' Suspected Rohingya Insurgents in Custody: Bangladesh Official," *Radio Free Asia,* April 18, 2018.

The Soufan Center, *The Nexus Between Human Security and Preventing/Countering Violent Extremism: Case Studies from Bosnia and Herzegovina, Niger, and Tunisia,* New York, March 2020.

Sude, Barbara H., "Prevention of Radicalization to Terrorism in Refugee Camps and Asylum Centers," in Alex P. Schmid, ed., *Handbook of Terrorism Prevention and Preparedness,* 1st ed., The Hague, the Netherlands: International Centre for Counter-Terrorism, 2020, pp. 238–269.

Sude, Barbara, David Stebbins, and Sarah Weilant, *Lessening the Risk of Refugee Radicalization: Lessons for the Middle East from Past Crises,* Santa Monica, Calif.: RAND Corporation, PE-166-OSD, 2015. As of February 16, 2021:
https://www.rand.org/pubs/perspectives/PE166.html

Swamy, Prakash M., "Sri Lankan Tamil Students Denied Admission to Educational Institutions in Tamil Nadu," *India Today,* February 15, 1992.

Syrians for Truth and Justice, *Deaths in al-Hawl Refugee Camp After the Outbreak of Typhoid,* Strasbourg, France, May 2018.

Taneja, Poonam, and Jewan Abdi, "Islamic State: Kurdish Forces Threaten to Stop Guarding Camps," BBC News, November 25, 2022.

Tayler, Letta, "Don't Let Orphan's Canadian Homecoming Be an Exception," Human Rights Watch, October 6, 2020.

Tayler, Letta, and Chris Albin-Lackey, "Kenya Recruits Somali Refugees to Fight Islamists Back Home in Somalia," *Huffington Post*, March 18, 2010.

Trisko Darden, Jessica, *Tackling Terrorists' Exploitation of Youth*, Washington, D.C.: American Enterprise Institute, May 2019.

Tsurkov, Elizabeth, "Uncertainty, Violence, and the Fear of Fostering Extremism in Syria's al-Hol Camp," *New Humanitarian*, August 27, 2019.

Tsurkov, Elizabeth, and Dareen Khalifa, "An Unnerving Fate for the Families of Syria's Northeast," Carnegie Endowment for International Peace, January 31, 2020.

UNHCR—*See* United Nations High Commissioner for Refugees.

United Nations, "Definition of the Term 'Refugee,'" Article 1A(2), in United Nations High Commissioner for Refugees, *Convention and Protocol Relating to the Status* of *Refugees*, Geneva, Switzerland, [1951] 2010, p. 14.

———, "Refugees Unlawfully in the Country of Refugee," Article 31(2), in United Nations High Commissioner for Refugees, *Convention and Protocol Relating to the Status of Refugees*, Geneva, Switzerland, [1951] 2010, p. 29.

United Nations Economic and Social Council, "Introduction: Scope and Purpose, Paragraph 2," in *Guiding Principles on Internal Displacement*, February 11, 1998, p. 5. As of May 14, 2021: https://undocs.org/E/CN.4/1998/53/Add.2

United Nations High Commissioner for Refugees, *The Situation of Palestinian Refugees in Lebanon*, Geneva, Switzerland, February 2016a.

———, "Flash Update: Iraqi Refugee Response in Hassakeh, Syria 18–25 October 2016," October 26, 2016b.

———, *Stepping Up: Refugee Education in Crisis*, Geneva, Switzerland, September 2019.

———, "Rohingya Refugee Response—Bangladesh—Operational Dashboard: 2020 Indicators Monitoring," infographic, July 31, 2020.

———, "Syria Emergency," webpage, March 15, 2021. As of May 14, 2021: https://www.unhcr.org/en-us/syria-emergency.html

United Nations Office for the Coordination of Humanitarian Affairs, "Syria: Humanitarian Response in Al Hol Camp," Situation Report No. 2, April 20, 2019a.

———, "Syrian Arab Republic NES Displacement Returns 18 Dec 2019," December 29, 2019b.

United Nations Office on Drugs and Crime, *Handbook on Children Recruited and Exploited by Terrorist and Violent Extremist Groups: The Role of the Justice System*, Vienna, 2017.

United Nations Relief and Works Agency for Palestine Refugees in the Near East, *Reconstruction of Nahr El-Bared Camp and UNRWA Compound*, Beirut, June 2012.

U.S. Department of Defense, Office of Inspector General, *Operation Inherent Resolve: Lead Inspector General Report to the United States Congress*, Alexandria, Va., April 1, 2019–June 30, 2019a.

———, *Operation Inherent Resolve: Lead Inspector General Report to the United States Congress*, Alexandria, Va., October 1, 2019–December 31, 2019b.

———, *Operation Inherent Resolve: Lead Inspector General Report to the United States Congress*, Alexandria, Va., January 1, 2020–March 31, 2020a.

———, *Operation Inherent Resolve: Lead Inspector General Report to the United States Congress*, Alexandria, Va., April 1, 2020–June 30, 2020b.

———, *Operation Inherent Resolve: Lead Inspector General Report to the United States Congress*, Alexandria, Va., October 1, 2020–December 31, 2020c.

———, *Operation Inherent Resolve: Lead Inspector General Report to the United States Congress*, Alexandria, Va., January 1, 2021–March 31, 2021a.

———, *Operation Inherent Resolve: Lead Inspector General Report to the United States Congress*, Alexandria, Va., April 1, 2021–June 30, 2021b.

U.S. Department of State, Bureau of Population, Refugees, and Migration, "Durable Solutions," webpage, undated. As of May 31, 2021: https://www.state.gov/other-policy-issues/durable-solutions/

"Video Claims to Show Islamic State Leader Abu Bakr al-Baghdadi Giving Sermon—Video," Reuters, July 6, 2014.

Watchlist on Children and Armed Conflict, "South Sudan: Briefing Note for the UN Security Council Working Group on Children and Armed Conflict," February 2015.

Widger, Tom, "Philanthronationalism: Junctures at the Business–Charity Nexus in Post-War Sri Lanka," *Development and Change*, Vol. 47, No. 1, January 2016, pp. 29–50.

Wilgenburg, Wladimir van, "One Woman Killed After ISIS-Motivated Riot in Syria's al-Hol Camp," Kurdistan24, September 30, 2019.

Wilkofsky, Dan, "In Syria's Deir ez-Zor, SDF Conscription 'Severs Livelihoods,'" *Al-Monitor*, February 22, 2021.

Williams, Katie Bo, "Coalition Plans to Expand Giant ISIS Prison in Syria," *Defense One*, February 24, 2021.

Wilson Center, "Syria," webpage, undated. As of May 14, 2021:
https://www.wilsoncenter.org/syria

———, "Timeline: The Rise, Spread, and Fall of the Islamic State," October 28, 2019.

World Health Organization, "Syria Crisis—WHO's Response in Al-Hol Camp, Al-Hasakeh Governorate, Issue 13, 2–15 August 2019," October 3, 2019.

Zelin, Aaron Y., *Wilayat al-Hawl: "Remaining" and Incubating the Next Islamic State Generation*, Washington, D.C.: Washington Institute for Near East Policy, PN70, October 2019.